OUT Our BACK DOOR

Driving Tours and Day-Hikes in Oregon's Coos Region

By Tom Baake

With Maps and Photos by the Author

Picnic spot along Elk River near Port Orford

Westways Press
Coos Bay, Oregon

OUT OUR BACK DOOR
DRIVING TOURS AND DAY-HIKES IN OREGON'S COOS REGION
Second Edition

WESTWAYS PRESS
440 Third Ct.   Coos Bay, OR   97420
(541) 269-5833

E-mail: *westways@harborside.com*
Web site: *www.scod.com/guidebooks*

When you travel any of the roads, trails and waterways discussed in this book, you assume responsibility for your safety. Author and publisher assume no liability for accidents and incidents. Every effort has been made to provide correct information but author and publisher cannot guarantee accuracy of information and cannot guarantee that tours are suitable for everyone and every vehicle. Please read important information in the Introduction.

Design consultation and printing by Wegferd Printing and Publications, North Bend, Oregon. Printed on recycled paper.
Cover photos: Hanging Rock along Panther Ridge Trail. (Chapter 21) Inset: Oregon Dunes National Recreation Area. (Chapter 7) Frontispiece and page 82 photos by Archina Davenport Page 10 photo by Iain D. P. Karroll

Library of Congress Cataloging-in-Publication Data:
Baake, Thomas C.
Out Our Back Door, Driving Tours and Day-Hikes in Oregon's Coos Region, second edition

ISBN: 0-9658012-0-9

1. Travel – Oregon
2. Hiking Trails – Oregon Coast and Siskiyous
3. Outdoor Recreation
4. Natural History   CIP: 97-90390

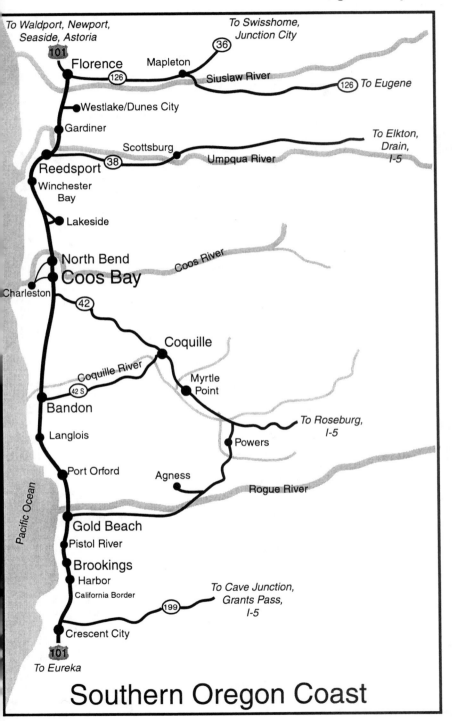

Southern Oregon Coast

CONTENTS

INTRODUCTION

Welcome to Oregon's spectacular South Coast! Exciting things are happening, with new areas open for recreation, new roads and trails for exploration, and improvements at many favorite destinations.

Yet it was the curmudgeon in me that originally inspired this book. Frustrated by crowds at the better-known sites along the coast, I began checking out some of the back roads and overlooked places. I was pleasantly surprised to find many quiet little spots to go for a picnic.

It's amazing how many interesting things you can do in this region. Ocean beaches, coastal bays and estuaries, the Oregon Dunes, rivers and waterfalls, lakes and forests, the miles of peaceful countryside and old roads . . .

This is great for visitors, of course, and perhaps even better for locals. You don't really have to make long excursions to see some of the scenic attractions that make Oregon so famous. They're right here, right in our back yard, "out our back door." You can sneak out for a little picnic, and be back by the end of the day!

For most of these outings, consider making a day of it, especially if you're inclined to stop occasionally, which I strongly advocate. Needless to say, a full fuel tank and a picnic lunch should be part of the plan. More about logistics in a moment. As noted earlier, these are intended as day trips, but many can be expanded to longer treks. I've included information about camping and other travel options.

While this is a book about back-road tours, it includes trips to the top scenic attractions. It's not fair to overlook them simply because they're popular. They're not *always* crowded!

Whenever possible, the driving expeditions are made into loops. You don't necessarily have to complete the loop, of course, and the drives can be approached from either direction. But there's often a reason for my recommendation -- views, for example, or an easier grade "going home."

The exceptions are chapters on local beaches, the Oregon Dunes, and South Slough National Estuarine Research Reserve. For those, a general overview is offered, with emphasis on walking options. Also included are in-town walks, as well as a chapter on hiking trails in the Siskiyou National Forest near Powers.

Some lonely roads are traveled in this book. There are details about road conditions and seasonal access, but you should always check with local sources about current conditions when traveling far afield. Weather-related closures and detours, budget crises and high forest fire danger can affect access.

Oh yes. . . about the weather. First of all, average rainfall is *60 inches* per year. It pours down -- or blows in sideways -- during awesome storms in winter and early spring. Trees are toppled, hillsides collapse, roads are closed, lowland areas are flooded. Yet it hardly rains a drop during July, August and September. We dry out and head to the other extreme — forest fire danger.

Then there's the wind. During most of the summer, you can count on wind from the north kicking up nearly every afternoon along the coast. Also fog in the mornings and evenings. Just a few miles inland, though, it can be a fine and warm and windless. That's where this book comes in handy, taking you from the chilly coast to an inland picnic where it's a nice day again.

Best time of year on the coast is Indian Summer, after the first rain or two. The wind has died down, the crowds have thinned out, and the light lies mellow across the land- and seascape. There's still plenty of warm sunshine for picnics. In winter, too, come interludes of almost balmy weather. The southern Oregon coast is frequently the warmest place in the state in wintertime, and there can be pleasant days of "false spring" that make you forget the weeks of dreary rainfall and gray skies. Indeed, so much of life on the coast is about the weather, and the weather's always changing.

Road Conditions
All tours in this book have been driven in a standard, two-wheel-drive family sedan. Most trips are on paved roads, sometimes with short stretches of gravel. A few are primarily gravel-road trips. You're not going to be comfortable negotiating some of the tours in an RV or towing a trailer. Remember that gravel roads get muddy, worse as winter progresses. In summer and fall they get dusty.

Several routes are closed by snow in late fall and winter, and are so identified in the "notes" section at the start of each chapter. *They should not be attempted when snowbound!*

Most importantly, many tours travel through working forests. That means you may encounter — as in coming at you head-on — fully-loaded log trucks, gravel trucks, water trucks, utility trucks, fire trucks, road graders or other heavy equipment. And as with any back-country travel, you'll encounter the occasional fallen rock and downed tree, but roads are rarely blocked for long

The single most important rule to remember is: ***just take it slowly***.

As for maps, those included in this book are all you need to complete the trips, but it never hurts to have more maps. Start with the State of Oregon highway map, then consider one of the privately produced regional maps. Chamber of commerce offices and info centers often have free "tear-off" maps.

U.S. Forest Service offices in Florence, Reedsport, Powers, Gold Beach and Brookings have maps for the Siuslaw and Siskiyou National Forests and for each respective ranger district. The Bureau of Land Management office in North Bend has detailed maps of BLM-managed areas. The combined Siskiyou National Forest/Coos Bay District BLM map is an excellent resource, available from either agency's offices.

A couple of the tours have their own guidebooks or brochures with maps, available from chamber of commerce offices, visitor information centers, county and state parks offices, the U.S. Forest Service and the Bureau of Land Management.

Map fever has soared to new heights with the use of global positioning satellite (GPS) technology, not to mention the advent of CD-ROM-based mapping software and Internet-available maps. Maps can be found at many places on-line, via government agencies and private sources, some of which are listed in the back of this book. There are errors and glitches in all of them. So I've worked hard to make the maps in this book as up-to-date as possible.

The best rule of thumb: when in doubt, stay on main roads. They'll lead you back to civilization. Every effort is made to maintain directional signs in the backcountry, but vandals, target-shooters and souvenir hunters wage a relentless siege.

Once again, remember that you're in a neck of the woods seriously intent on farming trees. Get ready to behold some formidable clearcuts, along with the systematic transformation of mixed-species forest into Douglas fir tree farms. No politics intended, merely a factual note.

That's not to say the grandeur is gone. It's just that it exists these days in what I call *islands*, and seeking them out takes a bit of venturing in the backcountry.

So let's venture to an island . . . and have a picnic.

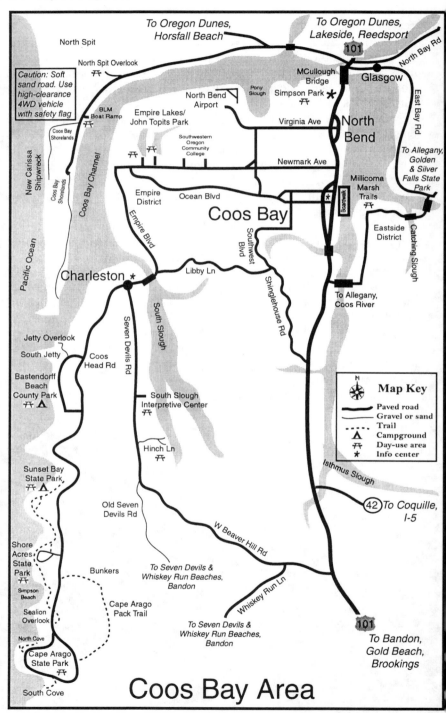

Coos Bay Area

PART ONE
The Coos Bay Area and Beyond

1. To the Cape: Sunset Bay/Shore Acres/Cape Arago

Road conditions: *Paved except for short side-trip on gravel road. Year-'round access.*
Notes: *30-mile round trip from Coos Bay or North Bend. Camping, day-use, hiking, fishing, boating, swimming, golfing.*

This is the best-known scenic tour in Oregon's Bay Area, and rightly so, since it gives you a real feel for the place along with some postcard-perfect views.

The route passes through Charleston, home of the commercial and sport-fishing fleet, and takes in three local treasures, the state parks at Sunset Bay, Shore Acres and Cape Arago. Along the way are picnic areas, fishing piers, campgrounds, hiking trails, a sea lion overlook, hidden beaches, tidepools, boat launches, RV parks and a golf course.

Highlight is Shore Acres, former estate of lumber baron Louis Simpson and one of Oregon's most popular state parks. Dramatically slanted sandstone bluffs receive a constant pounding by ocean waves, with especially spectacular results during winter storms. Not far from the relentless Pacific surge are clifftop gardens that flourish with seasonal and exotic plantings, best during the springtime rhododendron bloom. The adjacent rose garden, open summer and fall, is another sensual treat. At Christmas the gardens glow with hundreds of thousands of lights, and there are nightly activities.

In the spirit of this book, part of the trip is a loop, with a return through the hills of the local watershed.

Getting There
From US 101 in Coos Bay or North Bend, follow signs to Charleston, State Parks and Ocean Beaches. Roads merge at a "Y" intersection in Coos Bay's Empire district, heading west on Newmark Ave.

A pioneer-era settlement and the first county seat, Empire strives for revival, with a handful of businesses, shops, restaurants and nightspots. Newmark Ave. reaches the bay and turns left (S). One block farther west, down by the channel, is a boat ramp and fishing pier.

The road -- which changes names along the way from Empire Blvd. to Charleston Highway and eventually to Cape Arago Highway -- follows the shore past a gamut of residences ranging from the unkempt to the neatly kept, along with an assortment of RV parks, curio shops and small businesses. After about 4 miles a turn reveals the picturesque setting of Charleston.

Sandstone bluffs of Cape Arago slant up at dramatic angles. Observation building at Shore Acres State Park occupies former site of mansions of timber baron Louis Simpson.

Cross the drawbridge over South Slough and enter Charleston. There are shops, RV parks and cafes on the main drag, but for a look at the harbor, turn right (N) on Boat Basin Rd., which leads to the commercial fishing docks, charter boat operations and public boat ramps.

Here also are shops, restaurants, campground and RV parks, motel, charter boats, fish plants along with a Coast Guard station, Oregon Dept. of Fish and Wildlife office and the Oregon Institute of Marine Biology (OIMB).

A fisherman's memorial statue at the north end of the parking area overlooks the harbor; interpretive signs explain the function of various fishing vessels. There's always some sort of activity in Charleston and it's fun to just wander around on the docks, which are also open for crabbing.

Once you're ready to leave Charleston, get back on Cape Arago Highway and head west. The road goes uphill; to the left is Seven Devils Rd. (See chapter 4.)

About 1 mile west of Charleston, turn right (W) on Coos Head Rd. This way goes to a former Air Force "listening post" station now in transition to other uses. Just before the facility, turn right (N) on a gravel road.

The road runs along a fenceline. Keep left at the next intersection. Pass a whitewashed wooden navigational structure, used by ship pilots to get their bearings as they enter the channel. Round a bend and arrive at the Coast Guard watchtower. The view takes in the harbor's entrance -- or "bar" in local lingo -- with its rock jetties, as well as a spectacular stretch of coastline to the north, into the Oregon Dunes. You might also spot the stern of the shipwrecked *New Carissa* just offshore a couple miles north.

Return along the gravel road back to Coos Head Rd. Once to pavement in front of the former Air Force station, you have two choices:

1. Turn right (W) and go down to Bastendorff Beach and the south jetty. The road also leads to Bastendorff County Park, then back to Cape Arago Highway. (Winter note: the road is often flooded near the beach. You may have to double back.)

2. Or, turn left and return to Cape Arago Highway.

If you've chosen the second option, continue south on Cape Arago Highway. The second access to Bastendorff County Park and beach is in about 1 mile. Tucked up on the headlands are a campground, picnic tables and a big play area complete with wooden fort, slides, an old boat, spring-loaded dolphins and other such fun stuff. The beach offers walks in both directions, with the wave-swept jetty at the north end and a rocky peninsula and tidepools at the south end.

Continuing the tour from Bastendorff Beach, return to Cape Arago Highway and turn right (S). Pass one last stretch of private homes, then get ready to behold Sunset Bay.

The setting speaks for itself, get out and play. This charming little beach is protected from the surge of the sea by an offshore reef, and from prevailing winds by the headlands at either end, so it can be a calm refuge in every season. You might even see kids and other hardy waders splashing in the water on a sunny day. There are tide pools at either end of the beach, and Cape Arago Lighthouse (closed to the public) is on an island just north of Sunset Bay.

There's a group picnic area on the south end, with baseball field and volleyball courts. A sign commemorates millionaire publisher Malcom Forbes' transcontinental balloon voyage launched here in 1973.

Sunset Bay State Park offers camping and a hiker/biker camp. Just beyond is Sunset Golf Club, open to the public. A section of the Oregon Coast Trail (OCT) begins on the north side of Sunset Bay's picnic area, and continues out to the tip of Cape Arago. Short posts with embedded arrow symbols mark the OCT. The trail can also be picked up from most of the turnouts from here on out to the cape.

The road turns west, up through a vibrant slope of fern and forest, with the sea crashing down there on the right. Around a few turns is

Shore Acres State Park.

This was once the home of Louis Simpson, whose early-1900s timber empire bankrolled lavish estates on the spectacular, uptilted sandstone bluffs. His mansions boasted every modern convenience (the swimming pool could be filled with either salt or fresh water), and his fleet of sailing ships brought plants and cuttings from all over the world for his clifftop gardens. His first mansion burned in a spectacular fire on July 4, 1921, and the second one deteriorated beyond restoration and was razed in 1948, but some of the landscaping and a single garden house remained. The cottage overlooks an English formal garden that boasts beds kept bright with seasonal plantings ranging from daffodils and tulips in spring to late-bloomers like the showy dahlias. From early spring to mid-summer the intensely colored flowers of huge rhododendrons line the pathways, while blooming azaleas add even more color to the mix.

The walks lead to an Oriental garden laid out around a sunken pool complete with floating lilies, themselves a bit of show when in bloom. Even more unusual plantings ring the pond, and are identified with little plaques and signs. There are dwarf palms, a venerable-looking cherry tree, more rhodies, even a Zen-inspired "dry creek" of carefully-arranged stones And while the wind sighs through tall trees overhead and the sea crashes relentlessly in the distance, here in this garden, all is serene.

Beyond the pond, past hedges of rhodies, is the rose garden. It's open on a seasonal basis (when the flowers are in bloom, naturally). Even if you're not a rose person, stop for a smell!

On the site of the former mansions, out on the bluffs northwest of the gardens, is an observation building with pictures and displays. On days when the seas are high, the waves crash with awesome effect against the slanted rock formations here.

The road continues past Shore Acres. About 0.1 mile beyond is the northern terminus of Cape Arago Pack Trail. The 2.25-mile hiking trail heads up into the coastal hills and drops back down to the road at its terminus at the tip of Cape Arago. (More details at the end of this chapter.)

Next is Simpson Reef overlook, where you can spy on hundreds of sea lions and seals. The yowling critters swarm over Shell Island and offshore rocks, and feed in the rich waters of Simpson Reef. Migrating California gray whales pass close to shore here in spring and again in late fall, while orcas ("killer whales") can be spotted year-'round, even in estuaries.

Cape Arago is about 0.5 mile beyond. And it's all view beyond that! The sea takes up the entire horizon, with the coastline stretching off into the mists to the south. Paved footpaths to the north lead to picnic tables and a trail to North Cove (closed during seal pupping season).

There are more picnic tables and benches along the southern promontory, and a plaque on a rock here suggests that Sir Francis Drake in his ship *Golden Hinde* took refuge near here in 1579. As for the name, Arago (rhymes with "gotta go"), it's in honor of French physician and geographer Dominique Francois Jean Arago.

On the south end of the loop is the trail to South Cove, where there's a short beach and tidepools to explore. Try to visit these fantastic marine gardens at low tide.

A few hundred feet beyond, on a gated-off dirt road to a group camping area, is the southern terminus of Cape Arago Pack Trail.

Return the way you came on Cape Arago Highway to Charleston. You can opt for a visit to South Slough National Estuarine Research Reserve (see chapter 3) or take the Seven Devils Tour (chapter 4). Or return to North Bend or Coos Bay the way you came.

There's also an alternate way back to Coos Bay: Turn right (E) 0.5 mile past Charleston Bridge on Libby Ln. You'll catch glimpses of Joe Ney Slough, an arm of South Slough, down to the right. A commercial oyster farm has beds in the tidal flats.

The road curves up into the hills, through woodlands controlled by the local water company, which harvests the trees for additional revenue.

After 3 miles, the road crests, dropping down into a canyon once rich with coal. Few traces remain today, but Coos County's early-day coal industry supplied markets in San Francisco and beyond. Ore from seams here in the Libby district was loaded onto barges that had been floated up the appropriately-named Coalbank Slough, which lies before you as the road comes to a "T" intersection.

At the "T" intersection with Southwest Blvd. and Shinglehouse Rd., turn left (N), on Southwest Blvd., following signs to Coos Bay and US 101. The road weaves into the Englewood district, emerging on the south end of Coos Bay. Turn left (N) on Fourth St. to return to the downtown area, or to connect with US 101, four blocks east.

Cape Arago Pack Trail

Once part of a pack trail that led down through the rugged Seven Devils canyons to Bandon, this remnant section within Cape Arago State Park gives hikers a different perspective on the park -- and perhaps more appreciation for it, too. The trail can be approached from either direction, at its northern terminus near Shore Acres Botanical Gardens, or at its southern terminus at Cape Arago.

You can walk it out and back, of course, or return along the road, but conveniently enough, you can make a loop by connecting with the Oregon Coast Trail (OCT) that runs along the headlands.

The loop can be done from either direction, but I recommend a north-south trek in summer, so you'll have the wind at your back when you're out on the bluffs.

Park near the trailhead to South Cove on the loop road at Cape Arago. Walk up the road a few feet and turn onto a gated-off gravel road marked by a sign for Cape Arago Pack Trail. Go almost but not quite to the picnic tables in the group camp. Just before the camp, look to the right for a trail heading uphill. It's often missing its sign, but you can tell you're on the right track by the wooden waterbars laid in the trail. These diagonally-set berms carry rainwater off the trail, preventing ruts. Up we go!

The trail passes beneath tall, airy firs, up through the coastal trinity of Oregon grape, salal and huckleberry, some of the latter sprouting right out of ancient stumps. The trail tops out abruptly, then plunges into a canyon with a merry little stream. Just up-canyon are signs of logging beyond the park's boundary.

The path climbs again, then tops out for the final time along a 400-ft ridgeline. Just ahead, through a curtain of trees, are more logged-over slopes, which by now may have instilled that sense of appreciation for the park I mentioned earlier. Turn left (N), following a sign which if intact indicates this way to Shore Acres Gardens. The trail begins a delightful, slightly-downhill ramble through a corridor of towering trees. Depending on the winds, you may begin to hear the howling of sea lions, as well as the sounds of the sea. About 2 miles along, as the trail begins to head downhill, is an overlook with picnic table. Not far downslope, hidden in the brush to the left of the trail, are WW II-era bunkers that housed lookouts who manned various outposts along the coast here.

When you reach the paved road, turn left (S) and walk a few hundred feet, then turn right (W) onto a dirt road blocked off by posts. Follow this way west and you'll intersect the bark-lined OCT, marked by posts with arrows. Follow the OCT west as it heads for the bluffs, then turns south for about 0.75 mile, emerging by the sea lion overlook.

Cross the road just beyond the overlook to continue on the OCT, which rambles up into the woods before re-emerging on the road, where you'll walk the remaining 0.25 mile back to Cape Arago.

2. Easy Walks in the Coos Bay/North Bend Area

Road conditions: *Paved and sand. See notes.*
Notes: *Year-'round access. Paved, gravel, grass and dirt trails, including handicap-accessible. Day-use, swimming, boating, fishing, disc golf. Details of sand road vehicle access to New Carissa shipwreck and North Spit at end of chapter.*

The Coos Bay/North Bend area offers an ever-improving gamut of places for walks both easy and ambitious. In North Bend, you can stroll on a paved path that passes under the tall old trees of Simpson Park *and* the Art Deco arches of McCullough Bridge. Coos Bay has a waterfront walk, several little lakes with looping trails, and an estuary trail system in the Eastside district.

North Bend: *Simpson Park/Ferry Road Park Trail*: At the north

North Bend Trails

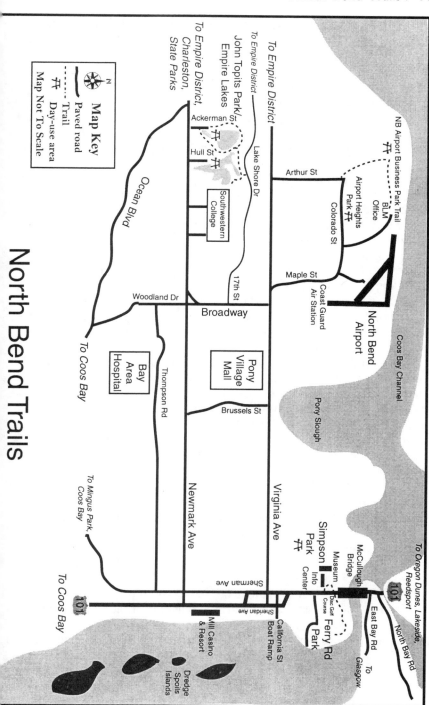

Map Key

— Paved road
···· Trail
ⓚ Day-use area
Map Not To Scale

end of town along US 101, by the "Welcome to North Bend" sign, in Simpson Park. The paved trail begins about 100 ft north of North Bend Information Center, on the west side of US 101. It goes under fine tall trees, untouched since the park's dedication by North Bend founder Louis Simpson in the early 1900s. The trail then swings under another local treasure, McCullough Bridge. Study the Art Deco-styled stairways and graceful support arches as the trails heads into Ferry Road Park. Among amenities is an 18-"hole" disc (i.e., Frisbee) golf course.

From Ferry Road Park you can walk down and look at the bay. Continue south through Ferry Road Park, and turn left (E) on Ferry Street, and follow the rough dirt road to the waterside. Before McCullough Bridge was built in 1936, ferries took passengers and vehicles from here across the bay to Glasgow.

Airport Heights: From US 101 in downtown North Bend, go west on Virginia Ave.12 blocks (about 1.5 mile) and bear right on Maple St., following signs to North Bend airport and BLM offices.

Continue past the Coast Guard air station and North Bend airport, following the road as it swings west, becomes Colorado Ave., and climbs a hill. Turn right (N) on Airport Ln., and follow it to the BLM offices. A trail begins where pavement ends. The blacktop stretch was relatively short at this writing, but more is planned, and you can extend your walk on connecting dirt paths.

The trail skirts behind a BLM warehouse. Just below is the city's wastewater treatment plant, airport runway, and beyond that, the bay channel. Across the water is Roseburg Lumber Co.'s dock and chip-loading facility. The paved trail heads uphill. Look for huckleberry plants on the left; they fruit in late fall and winter. Invasive plants such as Scotch broom and blackberry have taken a strong foothold.

Asphalt ends as the trail meets an old sand road. To the left is a way back to paved roads in the Colorado Loop area. Follow the sand track to the right, passing a WWII-era bunker, one of several underground shelters once hidden up here. The trail comes to a "Y." Bear right, following the main sand road. Side trails lead to blufftop overlooks guarded by picturesque, wind-sculpted shore pines. Here, too, are some tall firs and healthy-looking red cedars. Old alders grow thick beards of fluorescent-green lichen. The undergrowth is dense with salal, Oregon grape and some big rhododendrons. What a neat little forest, so close to town!

The trail comes to a "T" intersection, with both ways leading to residential neighborhoods. Plans call for extensions of the trail, but at this writing, the best option is to turn around and retrace your route. You could also make a loop by returning on city streets and sidewalks: east along Colorado Ave., then north onto Airport Ln. to the BLM office.

Coos Bay: *Boardwalk:* Start at pavilions along the waterfront adjacent to US 101 N, by Commercial St. A paved trail continues south from the pavilions, and takes in great views of the bay and town.

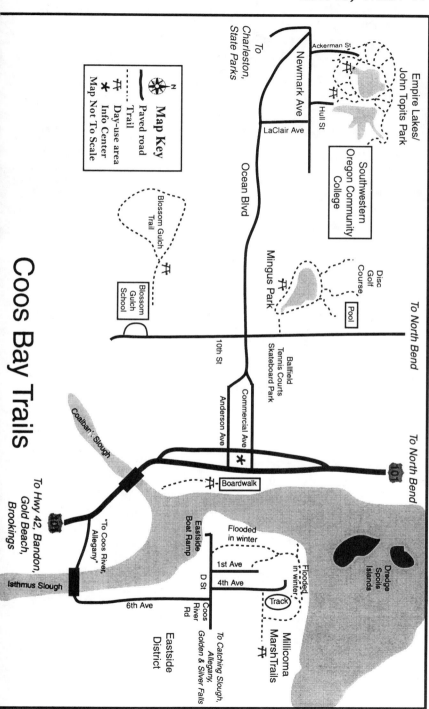

Coos Bay Trails

Wooden bridge spans an inlet of Lower Empire Lake

Mingus Park: From US 101, go west on Commercial St. for 8 blocks. Turn right (N) on 10th St., go 2 blocks to lake. There's a paved trail around the lake, and a network of gravel and dirt trails above the lake that connect to a disc golf course, swimming pool, tennis court, Boy Scout cabin, and residential neighborhoods.

Blossom Gulch Trail: From US 101 in downtown Coos Bay, go west on Elrod St. 7 blocks and turn left (S) on 10th St. In 1 block is Blossom Gulch School. Park at north end of lot and check in at office during school hours. The gravel trail begins along the northwest edge of the ballfield, west of the school, and continues along a stream and up onto the hillsides above the school.

John Topits Park/Empire Lakes: From US 101 in downtown Coos Bay, go north on US 101 1.7 miles and turn left (W) on Newmark Ave. In 1.8 miles turn right (N) on Hull St., following sign to John Topits Park/ Middle Lake. There are 4 miles of interconnected trails around the lakes. Most are paved. There are sandy beaches at both lakes from which youngsters have fun wading and splashing. The lakes are stocked with trout (and sometimes steelhead) and are open for year-'round fishing.

Millicoma Marsh: From the south end of Coos Bay along US 101, go left at the "Y," following the sign to Allegany, Coos River. Cross Isthmus Slough Bridge and go left (N) on 6th Ave. In 0.5 mile, at a "T" intersection, turn left (W) on D St. In 2 blocks turn right (N) on 4th Ave. Go 1 block, and go down driveway to parking area by track and ballfield. The trail begins at the south end of the track.

This is a popular bird-watching spot, and students from nearby Millicoma Middle School have built perches and boxes in many spots. Other poles hold curious-looking wooden houses for resident bats.

The trail heads east, with interpretive signs and overlooks along the edge of the estuary. Along this trail is a path to the north that loops back to the track in 1 mile. The latter trail also continues west to the edge of Coos Bay, although it's usually flooded in winter.

Port of Coos Bay Eastside property: This currently-undeveloped land near Millicoma Marsh belongs to the Oregon International Port of Coos Bay and was called White Point in the old days for all the bleached and broken clamshells in the soil. There were plank roads and docks, but now only a few rotted pilings at the water's edge remain. It's reverted to marshland sprouting a thick mantle of grasses, shrubs and trees, becoming a *de-facto* habitat for a wide variety of creatures. Birds, especially a huge congregation of noisy crows, are among the denizens. You can wander sand and grass-covered roads westward right to the edge of the bay, where your reward is a striking view of the Coos Bay waterfront.

As noted above, you can link to port property from the Millicoma Marsh Trail, although a key section of trail is usually flooded in winter. To directly access White Point, continue west on "D" St. and turn right (N) on 1st Ave. In the equivalent of 3 blocks (almost to the end of the street) is a sand road on the left (W), barred by an iron gate. Park off the road and walk west on the sand road. At a "Y" intersection bear right, and at a "T" intersection go left (W) to reach the bayside. You can get down onto tidal mudflats along here for more exploring.

(A right at the "T" intersection connects with the Millicoma Marsh Trail system, but as noted, this will be impassable by high water in winter.) Other old roads and trails wander around the property, but they're flooded in winter and early spring.

North Spit: In addition to trails in the Oregon Dunes discussed in Chapter 7, there are a few recreational opportunities on the North Spit, on the northern shore of the Coos Bay Estuary. There's a day-use area and short trail system at Weyerhaeuser's North Spit Overlook, a BLM boat ramp, and 4WD-accessible sand roads to both the *New Carissa* shipwreck overlook, and to the North Spit.

To get to North Spit from the Coos Bay/North Bend area, go north on US 101, crossing McCullough Bridge. About 0.6 mile north of the bridge, turn left (W) on North Spit Causeway, following signs to Oregon Dunes Horsfall Beach and Dunes. Cross the causeway, passing a Weyerhaeuser paper plant. Just across railroad tracks is a "Y," with the right fork to the Oregon Dunes. See chapter 7 for details.

Go left on Transpacific Parkway, following signs to BLM boat ramp and North Spit Overlook, 2 miles. The viewpoint sits atop a bit of high ground and takes in the coastal plain and a sweeping vista of the Pacific Ocean. To the south are the bayside towns, and to the southwest you might spot the *New Carissa* shipwreck.

A trail system begins on the northwest side, following old sand roads through the dunes and looping back to the parking area. Just below are ponds created for wildlife, with picnic tables and short, handicap-accessible trails.

Continuing on Transpacific Parkway is BLM North Spit boat ramp, and just past that, on the right (W), a sand road to the *New Carissa* shipwreck overlook. A Coos Bay Shorelands sign provides information. The sand road is open only to street-legal, high-clearance 4WD vehicles equipped with safety flag. *Caution: soft sand in summer!*

The Transpacific Parkway continues to a former aquaculture plant and dead-ends. A sand road, with the same restrictions as noted above, continues through shoreland forest and beaches to the North Spit. Signs provide more information, including tide charts *Watch for soft sand in summer, and be aware of tide times as portions of the road are submerged at high tide.*

What's a Coos?

Originally called Marshfield partly in honor of the town in Massachusetts and partly because it was built over mudflats, the town's named was changed to Coos Bay in the 1940s. As for the name Coos, Lewis and Clark referred to a place called *Cook-koo-oose*, named by Clatsop Indians. An 1828 explorer's journal called it *Cahoose*, later it was *Cowes, Koo'as, Kowes, Koos, Coose* and finally Coos, with Indian meanings varying from "place of pines" to "lake." At high tide, the bay indeed can seem like a lake, and probably seemed even larger in the era before dredge spoils islands and other fill projects.

3. South Slough National Estuarine Research Reserve

Road conditions: *Paved and gravel. Gravel and plank trails. Year-'round access.*

Notes: *25-mile roundtrip from Coos Bay. Day-use, hiking and canoeing/kayaking. Regularly scheduled group activities and tours.*

One of Coos Bay's premier back-door getaways is the South Slough National Estuarine Research Reserve. Set aside in the 1970s as America's first such preserve, South Slough offers a constantly-changing palette of waterways and tidelands surrounded by forest now protected from logging.

There are a handful of hiking trails and an interpretive center in the 4,800-acre preserve, but the best experiences are from a waterborne perspective. The Interpretive Center has a brochure and map with important info about tides and prevailing seasonal winds, and staff members can share up-to-date advice.

Canoe and kayak outings are scheduled on many summer week-

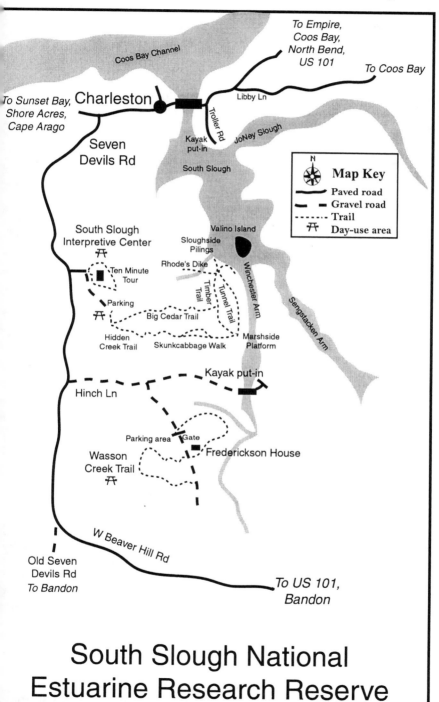

South Slough National Estuarine Research Reserve

ends, and other organizations such as the Audubon Society hold occasional tours.

Also offered at the Interpretive Center are brochures and maps about the hiking trails.

There are four basic walking tours at South Slough: the Ten-Minute Tour around the Interpretive Center, the Hidden Creek and Big Cedar Trails below the Interpretive Center, and the Wasson Creek Trail, accessible via Hinch Ln. 1 mile south of the Interpretive Center.

Getting There

From US 101 in Coos Bay or North Bend, follow signs to Charleston, Shore Acres State Park and Ocean Beaches. Refer to map to Charleston in the previous chapter.

From Charleston, head west on Cape Arago Highway. Just west of town, go left (S) on Seven Devils Rd., following signs to South Slough Reserve and Bandon.

The road curves uphill, passing Charleston Elementary School and the driveways of many tucked-away residences. Up along a ridgeline, the views open to logged-off miles of plunging canyons, with vistas west and south. (See Chapter 4 for more details of the Seven Devils route.)

About 4.3 miles along is South Slough Interpretive Center, with displays, information and friendly staff. Just below the pavilion is the "Ten Minute Tour," offering an overview of the slough and presumably spurring you to further exploration. Signs identify the brush and trees on the slope, in a state of regrowth following decades of logging.

From the Ten Minute Tour you can also link to the Hidden Creek and Big Cedar Trails down to the slough. Watch for signs. For direct vehicle access, read the next section.

A new trail is being planned to head north from the interpretive center, and may be completed by the time you visit.

Hidden Creek and Big Cedar Trails: From the interpretive center, drive down the gravel road to the right (S). You'll pass a "Y" with the left fork gated off; follow the right fork to a parking area. There's a big sign for the Hidden Creek Watershed Trail.

The footpath starts on the south side of the parking lot and heads downhill, switchbacking through thick undergrowth of salal, Oregon grape and huckleberry. Wild rhododendrons bloom here in late spring, and in fall the alders and other deciduous trees flush with color. During periods of summer wind, the tall evergreens sway with the breeze, but the canyon is sheltered.

You'll encounter a bench and interpretive sign, and get glimpses of the slough off to the south. Wooden bridges help with periodic crossings of Hidden Creek, and walkways and steps cross muddy areas.

Go right at a "Y" in the trail, continuing down a deeply shaded canyon, with another sign and more footbridges over aptly named Hidden

Skunk Cabbage Walk along South Slough's Lost Creek Trail

Creek. Next is a sign indicating the way to Sloughside Pilings via Skunk Cabbage Walk.

What fun! Raised wooden walkways zigzag through a sea of gigantic skunk cabbage. Alders rock gently overhead, shading the place in spring and summer. Their autumn show is splendid; in leafless winter their white bark looks like birch, stark and moody.

The walkway heads sloughward, out over marshlands thick with saltgrass, pickleweed and eelgrass. At the slough's forested edge the trail encounters the two-level Saltmarsh observation platform, with benches and interpretive signs. You can gaze on South Slough's Winchester Arm, and quiet study might reveal a stately heron or resting egret in its marshy reaches. While overhead the sheltering trees sigh and sway, sigh and sway . . .

Cross the platform and descend the other set of stairs to reconnect with the main path. At a "T" intersection, head right (E), following signs to Sloughside Pilings via Tunnel Trail, 0.5 mile.

The path heads uphill briefly, then levels out for an easy walk through thick huckleberry bushes -- you see why this is called the Tunnel! After about 12 minutes of walking, you'll encounter a rest room (a unique composting model, incidentally) and then come upon the Lookout, also aptly named.

If you're here in summer, the winds from the north may cool your enthusiasm, but make the effort to explore.

An interpretive sign explains the effects of dredging and diking here. The trail heads north, down stairs, then branches off. The trail to the east leads to three viewing platforms. The trail straight ahead (N) leads to the Sloughside pilings, while to the west is the trail to Rhode's dike. Each dead-ends at water's edge, offering close-up views.

Depending on the tides, you'll walk along dikes surrounded by a shimmering body of water, exposed mudflats laced with shallow channels, or something in between. The tidelands are dotted with shells and mollusks, and no matter what the tide or weather, you'll likely spot birds such as egrets and blue heron working the rich waters. The old pilings along here supported a frontier-era railroad trestle; the train took logs to nearby mills.

You can return the way you came on the Tunnel Trail, but for this tour, follow the Timber Trail, which begins near the bottom of the stairs below the Lookout and heads south, through another huckleberry corridor. After about 10 minutes of walking, you'll cross an old road blocked off by a wooden barricade. Just beyond that is a shortcut back to the observation platform. In a few more feet, turn right (W) on Big Cedar Trail, which immediately passes under some fine cedars. A catwalk with an interpretive sign spans a fragment of old train trestle. About 5 minutes of uphill walking brings you to the Big Cedar trailhead parking lot for group and handicapped access. Follow the road from the parking lot and continue uphill about 800 feet to a trail to the left marked by a "trailhead" sign. Follow it, and in another couple of minutes you'll intercept the trail on which you started. Follow it uphill to the parking area.

Wasson Creek Trail: From the Interpretive Center, go south on Seven Devils Rd. about 1 mile and turn left (E), on Hinch Ln. Follow this gravel road 0.8 mile to a road to the right marked by a sign with binoculars. Follow this road to a parking area. (The road straight ahead drops down to the slough and dead-ends near a popular put-in spot for canoeists and kayakers.)

From the parking area, you have two choices. You can start at the trailhead to the north, or follow the road/trail to the east. The trail to the north takes you on a 1-mile loop down to slough-level, then back up again past an old homestead, then up a canyon of mixed-species forest. You can forego part of the walk by heading east down the road to the old homestead, then up the Wasson Creek Trail.

The full loop: Just north of the parking area is a trailhead with sign and box that sometimes contains interpretive brochures. The footpath plunges immediately into a typical South Slough forest, with tall, spindly firs and cedars amid a sparse understory of huckleberry, salal and Oregon grape. There's a lot of woody debris on the forest floor, while massive old stumps attest to the size of trees that once grew here.

The trail heads gently downhill, then switchbacks to slough-level. At high tide times you'll see a ribbon of water, while low tides expose mudflats. The stillness is delicious. It's particularly reverential on a drippy winter day, all gray and hushed and somber.

You can find side trails to the water's edge, while the main path begins its uphill trek. Up through the forest and into a small canyon thick with ferns and grasses. It becomes a faint track momentarily, then suddenly you emerge into an old orchard, and here is the 1890s-era Frederickson home, looming all weathered and ghostly. The house is battened up to protect against vandalism, perhaps awaiting restoration, but it's fun to look at from the outside. A diamond-shaped window on the second floor is among the interesting touches.

The trail skirts below the house and then heads up to the access road. You'll see a sign with an arrow on it, pointing south. Follow it and you'll be on the access road for a few dozen yards before turning right onto Wasson Creek Trail.

This path traverses a showcase of South Slough flora: black currant, maidenhair fern, piggyback plant, red alder, red elderberry, evergreen blackberry, huckleberry, salmonberry, thimbleberry, salal and Oregon grape, all under a canopy of alder, fir, cedar, hemlock and large spruce trees.

In about 5 minutes the trail turns south, crossing a wooden bridge into a meadowy flatland. You can often spot elk and deer grazing in the valley's far reaches.

The trail crosses a bridge over Wasson Creek and heads into a stand of mighty spruce. These trees escaped the harvest of spruce in the Pacific Northwest during WW I. Tens of thousands of board feet of spruce was logged for airplane construction, but the war ended before the trees could be used.

The trail weaves through a maze of tree roots and heads back downstream through the woods. It emerges on the access road. Just across the road is an unmarked trail to a fish trap. Turn left (N) on the access road to return to the parking area. (You're welcome to wander southward along the road, which traverses more peaceful slough country.

Idyll of an Earlier Day

The Miluk Indians called this place *Tliyamani,* and found among the waters and marshes an abundance of life for food, clothing and shelter. They tended efficient fish weirs, dug up the many varieties of clams and collected other kinds of shellfish, and wove elaborate clothing, baskets and other goods out of fibrous cedar bark. They had an elaborate story-telling tradition, somber ceremonies and joyous celebrations, and even played a hockey-like game called Shinny on the tidal mudflats around today's Charleston.

They had accumulated centuries of knowledge about their environment, and knew not just what kinds of plants were good to eat or use for medicine, but when they were best to harvest. They incorporated such natural elements as white dentalium shells, feathers and blades of black obsidian into their clothing and jewelry, and were noted for their artistry in basket-weaving. The most prized baskets were so closely woven they could hold water, and were used as cookpots by adding heated rocks.

Among their myths was a prophecy that a "moving people" would come to change the ancient ways. The arrival of French trappers seemed benign enough, but an influx of white settlers in the 1850s seemed to fulfill the prophecy. At first, whites got along with the Indians. They bartered and traded; some even found wives among the Indians.

More settlers arrived; the pressure for land increased. In one of the darkest episodes in local history, the natives were rounded up and forcibly marched up the coast to a reservation.

Some hid from soldiers, others escaped to a fugitive life in the far corners of the forests and sloughs. White people were sympathetic to their plight, and helped Indians avoid authorities. Eventually, though, most ended up on the reservation, mixed together with many different tribes. After about 10 years the US government changed its policy again, closing the reservation and allowing Indians to return. By then, the "moving people" were pretty much entrenched, so Indians were given parcels of land as compensation. Other plans to repay Indians were attempted through ensuing years, some resulting in sweeping, nationwide changes, with litigation continuing to this day.

The 21st century brings a bit more recompense, along with recognition of tribes and the granting of additional territory. These original stewards of the land have managed to reclaim bits and pieces of their heritage, in the form of scattered parcels from the foothills of the Coast Range to the edge of the Pacific Ocean.

14. Seven Devils, the Sea and Thee: Seven Devils Tour

Road conditions: *Paved except for 4-mile section.*
Notes: *70-mile roundtrip from Charleston. Camping, day-use, fishing, boating.*

This tour starts in Charleston, home of the local fishing fleet, and heads south into terrain that bears the intriguing name Seven Devils.

Along the way is a stop at the South Slough National Estuarine Research Reserve, then it's on to some isolated beaches and a state park with historic lighthouse and more beaches. The last section gives a look at the lush farmlands along the Coquille River.

The trip involves less than 4 miles of gravel road, and there's an alternative "back way" if you want to avoid the gravel section.

Getting There

From US 101 in Coos Bay or North Bend, follow signs to Charleston, State Parks and Ocean Beaches. Refer to the previous chapter for more details.

From Charleston, head west on Cape Arago Highway. Just west of town, go left (S) on Seven Devils Rd., following signs to South Slough and Bandon. The road curves uphill, passing residences and Charleston Elementary School.

These days, Seven Devils Rd. eases along ridgelines as much as possible, and traverses areas opened up by frequent logging, but just imagine how rough the going was in earlier times. Pioneer accounts of Seven Devils date from to the original Hudson's Bay Company expeditions, and frontier explorer Jedediah Smith struggled through here in 1828. Smith's group journal called the route "pretty bad . . . thicketty and timbered, and some very bad ravines to cross."

How it came to be called Seven Devils isn't clear, for there are certainly more than seven steep canyons. Historians speculate the name has something to do with the expression "between the devil and the deep blue sea," this place perhaps being seven times worse owing to its ruggedness.

About 4.3 miles out is the South Slough National Estuarine Research Reserve interpretive center. The reserve takes in more than 4,800 acres of woodland and waterway, protected for study and limited recreation. The Interpretive Center has exhibits and information, and a helpful staff. At the least, take the 10-minute walk from the info center. (See chapter 3 for more details. Also in that chapter is info about South Slough's Hinch Ln. access 1 mile south of the Interpretive Center.)

Continuing past the interpretive center, proceed south on Seven Devils Rd. Recent logging has opened up some spectacular views of the ocean. About 2 miles from the interpretive center, the road bends sharply left

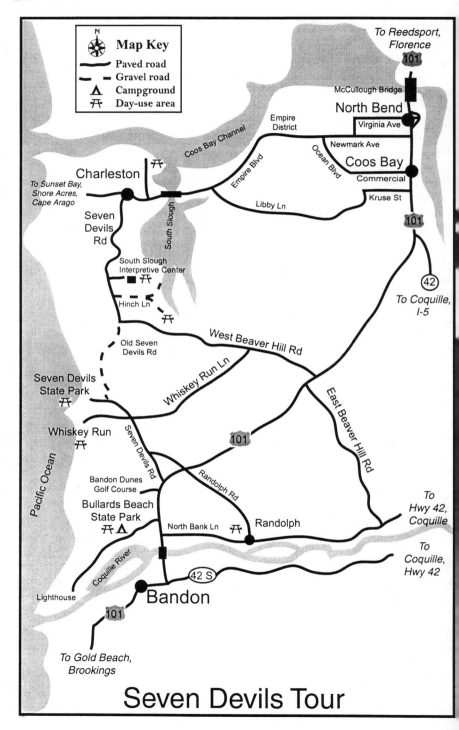

Seven Devils Tour

(SE), becoming West Beaver Hill Rd., and goes to US 101. For this tour, we'll head straight (S) on Old Seven Devils Rd. The road turns to gravel, passing clearcuts. The logging reveals expansive views south. The road twists down through the cutover canyons, finally plunging into standing timber. It's here among the tall trees you may get a sense of what the country was once like, and how arduous the journey through it.

Civilization reappears after 3.5 miles, in a valley with a few houses.

Pavement returns as the road swings up alongside a pasture, tops a rim of coastal benchland and becomes a straightaway running under a power line. In the next vale you'll encounter Seven Devils State Park.

This day-use area offers picnicking and access to Merchant's Beach, one of three long stretches of open beach in the vicinity. (For more details, see chapter 5.)

Continuing south on Old Seven Devils Rd., Whiskey Run Beach access road is about 1.5 miles. To get to Whiskey Run, turn right (W) and drive 1.3 miles to the beach. The setting isn't as nice as Seven Devils State Park, but the beach goes for miles in either direction, and there's vehicle access, if you're so inclined and equipped.

Gold found in streams trickling from the hills here in 1851 created a rush that eventually drew hundreds of miners. A town sprang up on the headlands, but storms washed away the beach gold in 1854, and subsequent fires wiped out every trace of the settlement.

These days the bluffs are strangled by gorse, a plant introduced by an early settler of Bandon. One look at this sea of thorny scrub -- whose

Peaceful meander along the lower Coquille River

seeds can lie dormant for years even if the plant is burned away -- may explain why some residents fear it will eventually dominate the entire coastal plain. Current measures to combat the spread of gorse include the introduction of a parasite that feeds on the plant.

How Whiskey Run got its name is another colorful story, though again not without dispute. Some historians say a cask of whiskey burst in an accident, causing miners to come running with all available pots, pans and cups. Another version has the cask broken open by a defiant evangelist.

Recreational miners occasionally work the stream with dredges or gold pans, and colorful stones can sometimes be found on the beach in winter and spring.

There was another flurry of activity at Whiskey Run in the 1980s when a windmill farm was set up, but nothing's left of it. A transpacific fiber optic line emerges from the sea here, serviced by a small control station.

Back on Seven Devils Rd., head south to US 101. At the highway, turn right (S). In 2 miles, just before the Coquille River, is Bullards Beach State Park. In addition to a popular campground complete with rental yurts, the park has picnic areas, a boat ramp, horse riding trails, a light-house and miles of beaches to walk. There's a pioneer cemetery on the headlands at the northern edge of the park.

Signs direct you to the lighthouse, which is open late spring to early autumn and has interpretive displays and photos.

Back on US 101, head south, and just before the bridge across the Coquille River, turn left (E) on North Bank Ln.

This is yet another peaceful byway of the region, and passes through a river valley routinely flooded by high water in winter and spring.

The road -- like most of the farms and homes -- sticks to high ground, and offers a palette apropos to the season: green and glowing in spring and summer; rich with autumn color; stark and muddy in winter.

The lowlands receive their annual flooding with apparently only ben-eficial effect, taking on fresh silt to emerge productive again for another season. Herds of dairy cows and beef cattle are moved around to ac-commodate the seasons. In late spring, summer and fall, you'll see them grazing in the lush lower pasturelands, while in winter they're brought to higher ground.

Just over 1 mile up is Rocky Point County Park, with picnic tables and boat ramp. Up around the bend is Randolph, fourth locale in Coos County to have that name. A handful of homes remain, and old docks and pilings stand as reminders of a community that once included saw-mills, shipbuilding yards, salmon canneries and a brewery.

North Bank Ln. continues above the fertile green plain, passing cus-tom homes, cluttered old farms and right through the middle of dairy ranches. You might have to wait for a herd to cross if it's milking time.

What are those cylindrical packages tightly bound in white plastic shrink-wrap? Hay bales, of course. It's the latest way to store them, to keep them dry!

Several historic roads that date to the time when there were coal-mining settlements in these hills have been marked by recent signs, such as Old Railroad Grade Road. They're dead-end roads, with not much to see along them, but what the heck, some people like to explore . . .

15 miles up, at North Bank Rd, turn left (NW) on East Beaver Hill Rd, following signs to US 101, Coos Bay, Charleston, Bandon.

The road climbs a steep but well-paved road for 2 miles to US 101.

Turn right (N) on US 101 to head back to Coos Bay. If you want to go back to Charleston on West Beaver Hill Rd. and Seven Devils Rd. (paved all the way; 14 miles), you'll see the turnoff to the left (W) just after you get back on US 101.

The road back to Charleston rolls over undulating hills of clearcuts and forest, passing the cutoff to the "old road" where you began this part of the loop. Stick to the paved main road to return to Charleston.

This is a fun little trek, not as complicated as it sounds. Rest assured everything along the way is very well marked, so give it a try, and don't be scared. There are only seven devils, after all.

5. To the Beach: Coos Bay to Port Orford

Road conditions: *Mostly paved. Year-'round access. Paved and sand trails. Some roads and trails subject to winter flooding.*

Notes: *Camping, day-use, hiking, fishing, boating, biking, horseback and OHV (off-highway vehicle) riding.*

Hey, it's just a trip to the beach, right?

Just a little walk along the water, maybe get a little wet, maybe watch the sunset. Sandy shoes, but everyone has fun. We can do this!

There are beaches close at hand and others that take some finding; those that are well known and a few usually deserted.

Wind, rain, fog, tides and a capricious sun conspire at all times. Meteorologists like to call it "maritime influence." It's always about the weather, and the weather always changes.

To the frustration of many visitors, summer can be a bummer on the Oregon Coast. Mornings may be foggy; almost always by afternoon the north wind has kicked in.

Everyone wants to at least *see* the ocean, of course, and hopefully get out for a little walk (or ride, if you're so equipped with dune buggy or OHV) but in many cases, the wind can quickly cool your enthusiasm.

(That's where this book comes in, by the way. Head inland a few miles and you'll amazed how quickly the fog and wind are left behind. It's a nice summer day again!)

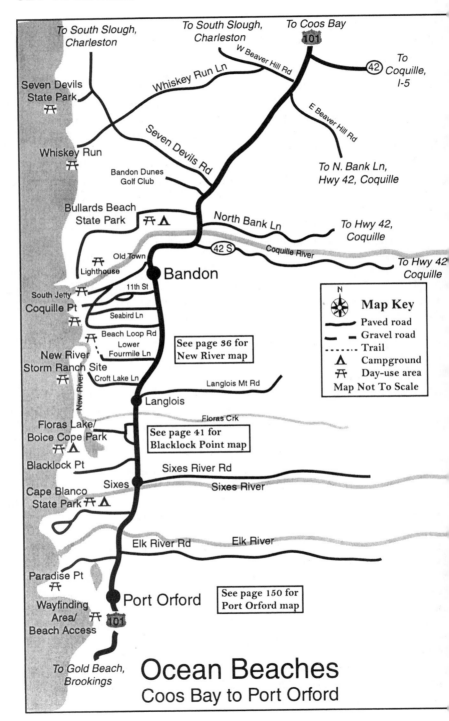

Ocean Beaches
Coos Bay to Port Orford

Best time for Oregon beaches is autumn, when the winds settle down and most of the visitors go home. It's still warm - - Indian summer warm -- and the light is golden and suffused.

In winter, coastal winds shift, arriving from the south and bearing frequent, ferocious storms. But there are nearly always a few periods of calm weather; in wintertime, the state's warmest temperatures are usually found on the south coast. Just remember you can get a sunburn even in January! And even on a cloudy day . . .

There's also something about the winter sun, arcing through its southernmost course of the year. It hangs low on the horizon, casting light at dramatic right angles, deepening shadows and adding depth to the land and seascapes. Winter sunsets come early, and can be among the most colorful, a rage of pinks and purples.

The winter ocean can be clean and blue, every breaker creamy with foam whipped up by recent storms. Incidentally, that foam is not the result of pollution, but the breakdown of algae and seaweed hastened by heavy surf and vigorous doses of storm-delivered oxygen.

The appearance of beaches changes with the seasons. High tides and winter storms beat right up to the foredunes and over, and some beaches wash away. Others lose much of their sand, becoming steeply slanted from water's edge to foredune.

It should go without saying that beaches must be avoided during storms. Every year people are hurt or killed by waves that hurl logs and debris onto the beach. Confine your storm watching to a safe overlook, such as the observation area at Shore Acres State Park, or even better, a room with a big window and a nice fireplace nearby. But let's not get too technical; any day it's not too windy is a good day at the beach.

Getting There
You're never very far from the seashore around here.

In the Coos Bay Area, the best known, most accessible beaches are Horsfall Beach, just north of the bay in the Oregon Dunes National Recreation Area, and Bastendorff Beach, on the way out to Cape Arago.

Horsfall Beach and other points north are discussed in the following chapter on the Oregon Dunes. For information about Bastendorff Beach, Sunset Bay and Cape Arago, see Chapter 1.

What follows is a general overview of beach access south of Coos Bay to Port Orford.

The coastline immediately south of Cape Arago is dominated by steep hillsides, with no beaches or public access, and appropriately named Seven Devils.

The next beaches are about 10 miles south, off Seven Devils Rd.

Chapter 4 has a tour to these beaches on Seven Devils Rd. beginning in Charleston. To access them from US 101 in Coos Bay or Bandon, here are directions:

From Coos Bay: Head south on US 101, and at the "Y" about 5 miles south, continue on US 101 following signs to Bandon. About 13 miles south of Coos Bay, turn right (W) on West Beaver Hill Rd., with signs to Charleston, South Slough, State Parks. In 1.7 mile, turn left (W) on Whiskey Run Lane, to Whiskey Run and Seven Devils Beaches. The road heads northwest, then goes west again as it drops down nearly to sea level. In 2.5 miles is a "T" intersection with Seven Devils Rd. A right (N) turn will take you in 2 miles to Seven Devils State Park. Or keep going straight (W) on Whiskey Run Ln. and you'll get to Whiskey Run Beach in 2 miles. Both beaches offer flat expanses of sand for miles in either direction. Vehicle access is allowed on Whiskey Run.

(Directions from Bandon: Head north on US 101. From the north end of Coquille River Bridge, continue 2.2 miles and turn left (NW) on Seven Devils Rd. In 3 miles turn left (W) and follow the road to Whiskey Run Beach, or continue north 2 more miles to Seven Devils State Park.)

Continuing south, the beach at Bullards Beach State Park invites further walks. There are three parking areas from which you can access the beach. The one farthest south is near the lighthouse and jetty.

Next is Bandon, about as good as it gets. The beaches start just south of the jetty, along Beach Loop Drive, and are some of the coast's most dramatic.

Offshore islands, called sea stacks, add to what's already a postcard setting. Five state parks are strung along Beach Loop Drive, all offering stunning views and beach access. Also along Beach Loop are motels, vacation rentals, restaurants, a few shops, a golf course and a horseback-riding stable. More details about Bandon and Bandon-area tours can be found in chapter 6.

New River

South of Bandon, US 101 follows an inland course, but there's an interesting twist on the beach scene at what's known as New River. This unusual, north-running river cuts off easy access to the Pacific Ocean, but parts of the river and surrounding land are protected as a Bureau of Land Management "Area of Critical Environment Concern," and there's another section set aside as a county park. The BLM area has some easy hiking and equestrian trails, picnic sites, a group center and a seasonally-accessible boat ramp.

New River is said to have been formed when a particularly wet winter in 1890 sent a lot of water down a coastal stream called Floras Creek. The creek carved a northward channel to find an easier way to the sea, and it's now about 10 miles long. This "moat" that effectively cuts off direct access to the ocean shoreline for part of the year (unless you have a boat, about which more in a moment.) Thus the ocean beach west of New River is said to be one of the least-visited on the Oregon Coast.

The Coos County Parks New River access is about 4 miles south of

Bandon, while the BLM's New River Storm Ranch site is about 8 miles south of Bandon.

Four Mile Dune Track: From the stoplight in Bandon at US 101 and 11th Ave., go south on US 101 about 7.3 miles and turn right (W) on Lower Four Mile Ln. The paved road turns to gravel in about 2 miles, and swings north. At this writing, the gravel road continues northward about 1 mile and ends at a barricade and parking area. A sand road (open to OHVs) continues another 0.5 mile to the edge of New River. The county plans to eventually extend the gravel road to the edge of New River, providing year-'round access to the river's north end

The county parks land encompasses 160 acres north of the road's end. Much of it is choked with gorse, but there are a few trails popular with equestrians and OHVers that roam through the low dunes. Vehicles are prohibited from crossing the river, and from driving on the beach.

Just north of the road's end is the usual summer/fall terminus of New River. It narrows into a tiny channel and disappears into the sand. During these periods, it's a simple matter to cross it at a narrow point and walk westward to the beach.

In winter and spring, higher volumes of water in New River push the channel another (approximately) 0.8 miles north before it turns westward and empties into the Pacific, effectively cutting off ocean beach access except to those with canoes or kayaks. *(Use caution when crossing New River in watercraft, and be alert for strong currents and winds.)* In times of heavy rainfall and high tides, New River may also breach the dunes near its confluence with Floras Creek.

BLM New River/ Storm Ranch Site: From the stoplight in Bandon at US 101 and 11th Ave., head south on US 101 8.7 miles. Just beyond milepost 283, turn right (W) on Croft Lake Ln. and follow its looping progress through forests, farms, fields and cranberry bogs. The road comes to a "Y" intersection in about 1.5 miles. Bear right, following signs to the BLM Storm Ranch site. The road turns to gravel near a bog and passes a gate and retaining wall as it enters BLM land. Next is the BLM interpretive area, on the site of the pioneer-era Storm Ranch. There are rest rooms, a group center and a camp host. A brochure, if available, offers a map and details of the walks. There's also an interpretive sign.

From Storm Ranch are short trails -- you can make them into loops- - for foot, bike, horse and wheelchair access. Some involve short uphill stints, and you can link to a trail that takes you to the edge of New River.

The River Road continues past Storm Ranch to the edge of New River, but there are seasonal closures to protect nesting shorebirds from March 15 to September 15, so you may have to park at Storm Ranch and walk the rest of the way to New River.

If River Road is closed: You can walk along River Road to New River, but if you're not portaging a canoe or kayak, consider taking the

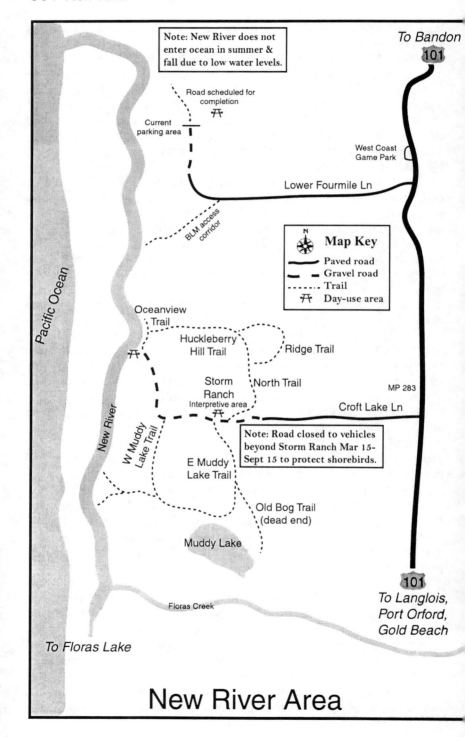

Note: New River does not enter ocean in summer & fall due to low water levels.

To Bandon
101

Road scheduled for completion

Current parking area

West Coast Game Park

Lower Fourmile Ln

BLM access corridor

Map Key
N

―― Paved road
- - - Gravel road
········ Trail
⊼ Day-use area

Pacific Ocean

Oceanview Trail

Huckleberry Hill Trail

Ridge Trail

Storm Ranch
Interpretive area

North Trail

MP 283

Croft Lake Ln

Note: Road closed to vehicles beyond Storm Ranch Mar 15-Sept 15 to protect shorebirds.

New River

W Muddy Lake Trail

E Muddy Lake Trail

Old Bog Trail (dead end)

Muddy Lake

Floras Creek

101
To Langlois, Port Orford, Gold Beach

To Floras Lake

New River Area

North Trail from Storm Ranch and connecting with the Huckleberry Hill Trail to get to Ocean View Trail and the picnic area beside New River. (See map.) You can return the way you came on the trails, or make a loop by returning on River Road.

If River Road is open: Continue west past the Storm Ranch site to a "T" intersection. To the left (S) is a closed road now part of West Muddy Lake Trail, which also leads to other New River overlooks. Turn right (N) and follow the road 0.3 mile to the end. There are rest rooms, picnic tables and boat launch. Canoes, kayaks and boats with electric motors are allowed on New River, but no gasoline-powered motors are permitted. *(Use caution when crossing New River and be alert for strong currents and winds.)*

At the northeast corner of the parking area is access to Ocean View Trail, which rambles through coastal forest to a couple of New River overlooks, and connects to Huckleberry Hill Trail back to Storm Ranch.

Trails from Storm Ranch: (These are for hikers and equestrians, since the sandy footing makes biking difficult.) From the interpretive sign, follow North Trail along an old road (north of course), skirting open meadows and spindly manzanita bushes. The road narrows to a sandy track, and heads uphill. The forest floor here and in many parts of the New River area is carpeted with mosses, fungi and lichen, the latter of which has an almost-florescent lime-green color.

At a "T"intersection you can go right on Ridge Trail for a short loop back to North Trail, or you can continue on North Trail as it turns into Huckleberry Hill Trail. The shore pines and Sitka spruce close in and the dunes help muffle sounds, and although you can still hear the ocean, there's a sense of peaceful isolation back here.

Follow trail markers as the path weaves through the small, overgrown dunes, some of which afford views of the surrounding area. The forest floor hosts understory of salal, Oregon grape, huckleberry and occasional rhodies. You'll come to a "T" intersection with Ocean View Trail; turn left (S) and follow it to the parking area near New River. Side paths off Ocean View Trail offer views of the river.

You can retrace this route back to Storm Ranch, or follow River Road back to the interpretive site.

Muddy Lake Trails: (Open for hikers, equestrians and mountain bikers, this trail also has a portion accessible to wheelchairs.) Muddy Lake Trail provides another perspective on the New River area, as well as a view of Muddy Lake. Look for the parking area on the south side of River Road not far beyond Storm Ranch. The path crosses a footbridge and heads up an open meadow, with wind singing through the shore pines and the sea sounding quite nearby.

You'll pass the intersection with Old Bog Trail, which climbs up to a short ridge before dropping down near an early-day cranberry bog and the edge of Muddy Lake. In recent years the Old Bog Trail continued

A view from New River's north end

westward around the lake (and a sign at the trailhead may still indicate this) and connected with the Muddy Lake Trail, but don't bother trying, as the lakeside trail has been swallowed up by mud and is seriously overgrown by brush. If you've taken the Old Bog Trail as a little detour, just turn around and double back to the East Muddy Lake Trail.

Continuing on East Muddy Lake Trail, you'll descend through a forest corridor to emerge near the shore of Muddy Lake. Approach quietly, as birds are often resting on this shallow lake.

Indeed, the first things you may notice when you visit the New River area are the birds -- ducks and geese and a busy gamut of shorebirds. The unmistakable cry of an eagle; a blue heron rising suddenly from a feeding spot along the waterline. If you're lucky, maybe you'll see more exotic varieties such as peregrine falcon.

From the edge of Muddy Lake, follow the gravel road west to a "T" intersection. The old road ahead leads to New River overlooks; a turn to the right (N) takes you back to River Road, which you can then follow eastward back to Storm Ranch (or north to the edge of New River.) Retrace your vehicle route to US 101.

A Detour in Langlois

Farther south on US 101 is Curry County, which boasts many, many miles of open beaches. I'll discuss a couple at the north end of the county in a moment, but let's pause for a moment in Langlois, 14 miles south of Bandon.

Hub of a once-bustling sheep and dairy region, Langlois today is home to a handful of stores and galleries along with the requisite cafe (actually called "The Greasy Spoon") and general store.

The Rain Coast Art Gallery is in the old Woodsmen of the World building, a classic, two-story frontier-era structure that was the site of many early-day gatherings.

Once called Dairyville, the town was renamed for a prominent Curry County family. William Langlois came from the Isle of Guernsey in 1854, following the California Gold Rush. His son Frank continued the dairy and mercantile operations, and another son James, was Cape Blanco Lighthouse keeper for 42 years.

Across US 101 from the general store is Langlois Mtn. Rd., well worth a little detour.

The road dead-ends after about 8 miles, so there's no need to drive it all, but head up for a mile or two. And I do mean UP. This is as close to an airplane ride as it gets (and much cheaper). The views stretch north to Cape Arago and south to Cape Blanco, and below is the coastal plain, glistening with lakes and sinuous rivers.

You can turn around at an old rock quarry as the road tops off along a ridgeline, but if you're interested in continuing, the road keeps rolling through the grassy slopes, swooping down into pocket valleys, passing ranches and residences and an old "wigwam" burner at a former saw-mill site. In pioneer times, the road continued over to the Coquille Valley, but as mentioned now ends at private ranch roads.

Floras Lake/Boice-Cope Park

Back on US 101, just south of Langlois watch for signs to Floras Lake and Boice-Cope County Park. Turn right (W) on Floras Loop Rd, and follow signs to Floras Lake. The road zags through farms and ranches. If you're here in summertime, you'll understand why Floras Lake is a premier windsurfing spot on the coast. The wind will probably be blowing steadily; if it's not or you're here in some other season, just look at those bent and wind-sculptured trees if you want to know how cease-less is that summer breeze.

There's a big bed-and-breakfast just before the lake, with a windsurfing resort and a smattering of custom homes to the south. Curry County operates a campground, and asks for a day-use fee if you want to park in the lot next to the lake. There's a boat ramp, but windsurfers, canoe-ists and kayakers like to use another launch point a bit to the south, accessible from the campground.

Signs explain this was once called Lakeport. Developers in 1910 had the idea of digging a channel between the lake and the sea and creating a port. The lake itself is deceptively large -- 25 square miles -- and very deep, and the scheme seemed plausible enough. In addition to Lakeport, a town called Crittenden was platted, and extensive orchards were planned for the coastal plain to the south. The idea was for settlers to buy a plot in town that included title to part of the orchards.

More than 400 people were drawn here, and it was said 200 of them were employed at a sawmill and in related concerns. There were businesses, saloons, a newspaper and a three-story hotel. When it was discovered the lake was higher than the sea, and would drain away if the channel were dug, the plan -- and the town and its people -- likewise drained away.

In modern times the lake was discovered by windsurfers, and they add a colorful presence.

From the day-use area are easy trails to the beach, and the area is closed to motor vehicles so you don't have to worry about being run over by a dune buggy. The North Trail is a mere quarter-mile, and offers access to the beach northward. The South Trail meanders for about 1 mile along the edge of Floras Lake before hitting the beach at the south end of the lake.

Access to parts of the beach and foredunes are restricted from March 15 to September 15 to project snowy plover, a threatened shorebird.

This is definitely not the easiest beach to walk on the Oregon Coast. In fact, it's one of the steepest beaches, and the sand is soft and slow going, even at the water's edge. You could, however, walk the beach north all the way back to Bandon, although that would require fording several streams that can get large and dangerous in times of heavy rainfall and high tides.

The trail to the south along the edge of Floras Lake leads to South Beach, a small beach with equally soft sand. It's covered during high tide, and its southern progress eventually ends at the headlands of Blacklock Point.

At South Beach you can connect with the Oregon Coast Trail (OCT) heading south toward Blacklock Point, and with another trail on an old road to Cape Blanco (Sixes) Airport. More on these trails in a moment.

Returning to the road at Floras Lake, retrace your way back on Boice-Cope Rd. and then Floras Lake Rd. At the intersection with Floras Loop Rd., turn right (S), following it past a pioneer cemetery and back to US 101. To continue this tour, turn right (S).

Blacklock Point

This is another overlooked treasure, one of the most wild and remote locales on Oregon's South Coast. Part of a minimally-developed state park, Blacklock Point has hiking, mountain biking and equestrian trails that lead to inspiring headland vistas, while nearby features include a picturesque, secluded beach as well as an unusual waterfall that cascades off coastal headlands and plunges 150 feet into seaside rocks.

Most of striking of all is the sense of isolation. The forests range from tall firs and Sitka spruce to stunted, wind-sculpted shore pines that look like something out of the Hobbit. (The latter is actually referred to as a pygmy forest.) The denser parts of the forest have a spooky look

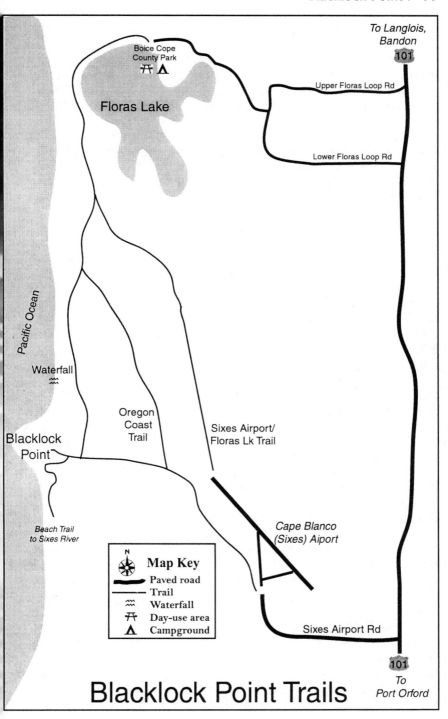

To Langlois, Bandon
101

Boice Cope County Park

Floras Lake

Upper Floras Loop Rd

Lower Floras Loop Rd

Pacific Ocean

Waterfall

Oregon Coast Trail

Sixes Airport/ Floras Lk Trail

Blacklock Point

Cape Blanco (Sixes) Aiport

Beach Trail to Sixes River

N
Map Key
Paved road
Trail
Waterfall
Day-use area
Campground

Sixes Airport Rd

101
To Port Orford

Blacklock Point Trails

that reminds some visitors of the forest in *The Wizard of Oz*, but don't worry, they won't try to grab you!

The forest understory is jungle-dense in places with salal, Oregon grape and huckleberry, while wild rhodies bloom in such profusion along the trails in late May and early June you may think they were planted! Other parts of spring and summer bring smaller yet equally delightful wildflowers into the picture.

Most trails angle through the flat coastal benchlands along old jeep roads, which unfortunately contain some huge potholes that can be filled with water even into late summer. Elevated wooden walkways traverse the worst areas, but there are many other muddy places, so do this trek in waterproof footwear. If you're biking, be prepared to get muddy, or perhaps save this for late summer or fall.

Getting There: About 5.5 miles south of Langlois (10.5 miles south of Bandon), turn right (W) on Cape Blanco Airport Rd., Curry County 160. It's directly across from Pacific High School. Follow the road 2.8 miles to a parking area adjacent to the airport.

A sign points the way to Blacklock Point, Floras Lake, and the Oregon Coast Trail (OCT). Head northwest on the trail. You'll pass side trails and old roads to the left, but continue NW. The trail parallels the runway; you can glimpse it off to the right as you hike along. In about 0.75 mile is a stream crossing. Just beyond that is a "T" intersection. Go left (W).

The next intersection is marked with a sign; turn left (W) toward Blacklock Point. You'll encounter boggy areas and the raised walkways. At the next junction turn left, following the sign to Blacklock Point. The sounds of the sea by now should be urging you on, and in a few minutes you'll come to a campsite under some big sheltering Sitka spruce, and just beyond that, the meadowy headlands of Blacklock Point.

On to them! The horizon fills with an absolutely thrilling spread of Pacific Ocean, while closer at hand waves roil and foam against landward rocks. To the south is a sweet curve of beach framed by coastal forest, with Cape Blanco's distinctive point and blinking lighthouse in the distance.

Footpaths out to the bluffs lead to overlooks of the barren, crumbling-gray rocks of Blacklock Point. You might spot tangled and rusted iron beams from a railroad that once ran along Blacklock Point for a quarrying operation. According to Port Orford writer Neonta Hall, before the year 1900 a total of 18 public buildings in San Francisco were faced with Blacklock Point sandstone.

The trail to the south beach begins just as you emerge from the campsite area onto the headlands. It switchbacks down to the beach, and from there you can walk south to Sixes River, about 1 mile. In low-water times of late summer and fall, it's possible to ford -- with caution -- Sixes River and connect to trails to Cape Blanco State Park.

Wildflowers and lonely beaches of Blacklock Point

To check out the waterfall, return to the last intersection and follow the OCT north to Floras Lake. In about 10 minutes you'll notice a well-traveled spur to the left (W), which leads to sandy-colored bluffs and the 150-ft. cascade. *Be extremely careful near the unstable edges of the cliffs!* If you're here in summer, when the wind pushes in from the north and the waterfall's flow is low, you might marvel at the sight of water and mist being blown back up in a rainbow spray over the lip of the waterfall.

Back on the main trail, you can return to the parking area the way you came in. To make a bit of a loop of this walk, continue north toward Floras Lake and at the next junction in 0.5 mile, turn right (S). This will connect you, in about 1 mile, to the trail you came in on, for a return to the airport.

You can continue on the OCT north to Floras Lake, where you can also connect with a 3-mile trail back to Sixes (Cape Blanco) Airport. This route follows an old road and is fairly flat and featureless, traversing a corridor of trees and tall brush.

The OCT along here is really nice as it slowly descends from the forested headland to the benchlands near Floras Lake. Gently down we go, until the headland gives way to South Beach, where a creek enters the ocean through a cleft in the last bit of bluff. Scramble down the trail, cross the creek and pick up the OCT as it heads back uphill, and shortly you'll be overlooking Floras Lake. There are beach closures in an area near South Beach from March 15-Sept 15 to protect snowy plovers. The OCT follows the lake's edge, passing a short trail to North Beach (unaffected by seasonal closures), and to the day-use area and campground at Boice-Cope County Park. (The beaches here are some of the steepest on the Oregon coast. The sand is soft and the walking is slow going!)

Cape Blanco State Park

You could easily spend a whole day enjoying Cape Blanco State Park, just north of Port Orford. In addition to tours of a restored pioneer-era ranch house and of the Oregon Coast's oldest lighthouse, there are hiking and equestrian trails, as well as beaches and coves to explore, many picnic places and a year-'round state parks campground.

Getting There: From Bandon, go 22 miles south on US 101 and turn right (W), following signs to Cape Blanco. (Cape Blanco is 3 miles north of Port Orford.)

This is one of the coast's windiest locales, as evidenced by the low-lying brush and sculpted trees. It can be downright nasty out here, with extremes of harsh winds and lashing rain. But there's one trick to keep in mind: in summer, the wind arrives from the north, so the south side of the cape can be pleasant. In winter, the wind comes from the south, so try the trails on the north side.

The road to the cape rolls through windswept coastal benchlands and in about 4 miles encounters historic Hughes House, restored and open for tours by volunteers (April 1 – Oct 31, 10 a.m. to 3:30 p.m.; closed Tuesdays and Wednesdays).

Patrick and Jane Hughes were among the earliest white arrivals, settling here with a handful of fellow Irish immigrants and establishing a homestead, dairy farm, even a Catholic parish. Said to be the best-preserved Victorian home in Curry County, the house was built in 1898 and was part of a working ranch for 111 years. Period furniture decorates many rooms, and the restored pioneer-era kitchen is among projects representing many hours of volunteer labor in recent years.

There's a day-use area along the river, with a boat ramp. Narrow stretches of the river are popular for bank fishing during salmon and steelhead runs. A trail heads west along the river and connects with other trails to the headlands and to North Beach.

The road continues from Hughes House, passing a pioneer cemetery with a half-dozen markers. Down the road 0.3 mile from the cemetery is a road to a horse staging area and campground for "horse people," with access to a horse/hiker trail. The gravel road ends at the main campground, with access to South Beach, about which more in a moment.

Just across the road is Pacific View Trail, which leads in less than a half-mile to some terrific headland views, and to a connection with a trail to Hughes House.

Sticking to the main road, the state park campground is in another half-mile. Just ahead is the lighthouse, and just across the road from the campground entrance is South Cape Trail, to yet more profound vistas.

It's usually pretty windy out here, but if you luck into a calm day (or perhaps at sunset when winds sometimes die down), check out the picnic tables along South Cape Trail. In addition to those stunning views, summer brings a luxuriant sea of wildflowers to envelop the tables.

The state park campground is set amidst heroically sighing pines and spruce, the crashing sea sounding mere feet away. You can drive through the campground to get to South Beach. (Info in a moment.)

The main road ends just west of the campground, with the lighthouse looming. As noted, this is the oldest (1870) and tallest (59 feet) light on the Oregon coast. Now automated, it casts a beam seaward 22 miles, and a radio signal 250 miles. Restored and staffed by volunteers, it's open for tours April 1 – Oct 31, 10 a.m. to 3:30 p.m.; closed Tuesdays and Wednesdays.) A first-floor display has photos, artifacts and interpretive information.

From road's end you can pick a path down to a beach on the north side of the cape and walk up to the mouth of the Sixes River. Other trails follow the headlands south, and South Cape Trail also offers picnic tables and benches in romantic settings.

You can drive close to South Beach -- and onto it, if you're so inclined and have a high-clearance 4WD vehicle -- via an access road out of the campground. Follow signs to the beach.

South Beach is another long, level stretch of sand made cozy by a frame of timber running along the terraces above it, while imposing Orford Heads looms in the distance. The Elk River's confluence with the sea is about 2 miles south. Lining the riverbank and adjacent beach are a multitude of colorful rocks and the occasional agate. It's usually pretty easy to cross Elk River, and in summertime the mouth is often completely sanded in, or "bar bound," in local lingo. Autumn rains eventually open the river, letting in salmon and steelhead that have been waiting offshore to make their fall run upriver to spawn.

From Elk River, the beach continues south another 2 miles to Paradise Point, and from there to the feet of Orford Heads. (You can also drive to Paradise Point; take Paradise Point Rd. off US 101 just north of Port Orford.)

There's an excellent beach in Port Orford, too, accessible from the Battle Rock Wayfinding Area at the south end of town. Vehicles are permitted on the beach.

Here we reach the southern limit of this guidebook (with the exception of details about Humbug Mountain State Park in chapter 24.)

But the beaches go on and on and on . . .

6. Bandon Area Tours

Road conditions: *Paved. Year 'round access.*
Notes: *Walking and driving tours of beaches and back roads in the Bandon vicinity. Stay off beaches during winter storms. Summer afternoons bring north winds.*

A bit about Bandon: At least three Indian encampments have been identified near the mouth of the Coquille River, but when whites settled in this area, they focused first on the gold-rich sands up the coast at Whiskey Run, or at such riverside settlements as Randolph and Parkersburg. Bandon was established in 1874 as a separate precinct from Randolph by George Bennett, member of a prominent family from Bandon in County Cork, Ireland. Through the ensuing years the town boasted sawmills, salmon canneries, shipyards and a woolen mill.

Although some historians question his right to such a title, George was called Lord Bennett. While he and his family did much to establish Bandon, he's most remembered -- reviled would be more like it -- for his introduction of gorse, or Irish furze, a thorny and remarkably hardy shrub. Gorse defies eradication; its seeds are not even destroyed by fire and can lie dormant for *30 years*. Along with the equally invasive scotch broom, the plant blooms with bright yellow blossoms in spring. Visitors frequently ask what the pretty yellow plants are, and get the answer through clenched teeth.

To make matters worse, gorse is high in flammable oils, always a threat during fire season. A particularly dry year in 1936 brought such fires, one of which got out of control with terrible consequences, burning many of the homes and completely destroying the downtown and water-front of Bandon but for two structures.

The town was gradually rebuilt, and in the 1980s an ambitious project fueled by federal dollars helped recreate Old Town and build the water-front marina. In addition to many shops, galleries, restaurants and of-fices, you can check out the survivors of the '36 fire: the Masonic Temple at Second St. SE and Alabama, originally a bank and in recent years a cobbler's shop; and the Breuer Building, 460 First St. SW on the road to the south jetty. Ironically, this was originally a cobbler's shop, and now sits alongside some other fine old buildings, including the former Coast Guard station, a tidy, whitewashed two-story building constructed in 1939.

Development in Old Town Bandon continues, with a new waterfront boardwalk -- called the Riverwalk -- beginning near the marina and ex-tending westward. There are public docks for fishing and crabbing.

Bandon-by-the-Sea -- a name coined to capitalize on the town's ob-vious assets -- has long attracted visitors and retirees, but it has another thriving industry in the form of cranberries, which grow in more than 2000 acres of bogs from Port Orford to just north of Bandon. The town's main event is the Bandon Cranberry Festival in late September.

Although Oregon has a cranberry native to its marshy boglands, the cultivated variety was introduced in 1885 from Massachusetts, and the "bogs" are now carefully sculpted basins kept watered by an elaborate system of irrigation canals, wells and pumps.

During the autumn harvest season, the bogs are flooded, bringing the berries to the top of water where they're scooped out by workers driving specially designed machines. You can see many of the bogs from US 101. For an interesting drive (or bike ride) that takes in closer views of the bogs, head south from Bandon on US 101 and take a left (E) turn on Two Mile Ln. Follow it 0.7 mile to Rosa Rd. and turn left. Rosa Rd. passes many bogs as it rolls 3 miles north to an intersection with 11th Ave. Turn left (W) to return to US 101.

Other Bandon industries including a dairy cooperative famous for its Bandon Cheese Factory, located along US 101. You can sample a couple of dozen cheeses, watch a video on the cheese making process and view some of the equipment and activity through windows into the plant.

Cranberry Sweets, located in Old Town Bandon across from the waterfront, offers a chance to watch candy making, while Bandon Glass Art Studio along US 101 across from Old Town has frequent demonstrations of glass blowing. There's another glass blowing studio about 4 miles south of town on US 101.

Just a block south of the cheese factory on US 101 is the Coquille River Museum, located in the town's former city hall. Here you'll find early-day photos and artifacts, as well as exhibits on such subjects as cranberry and dairy farming, logging and mining, fishing and shipwrecks.

Beach Loop Drive: Bandon is perhaps best known for its beaches, which are some of the coast's most awe-inspiring. No trip is complete without a tour of Beach Loop Drive, which features five state park day-use areas with beach access. There are many custom homes, along with motels, restaurants, vacation rentals, the Inn at Face Rock Golf Course, and horseback riding stables.

Begin a tour from Old Town, and head west along the jetty road. The first beach is actually at the end of Jetty Rd., which is also a popular spot to watch the waves lash against the rock jetties. *Do not go on the jetty in rough weather!*

Follow signs from Jetty Rd. to get to Beach Loop. You'll start on Edison St., which heads up the hill from the river area. Turn right on 4th St., which turns into Beach Loop Drive as it heads seaward. Passing many residences, the road comes to a stop sign at the intersection with 11th St. Turn right (W) to get to Coquille Point, where there are short headland trails and a fancy wooden stairway down to one of the best of Bandon's beaches. Here are the famous seastacks, so picturesquely situated just offshore.

Continuing south on Beach Loop Drive, you'll pass four more state

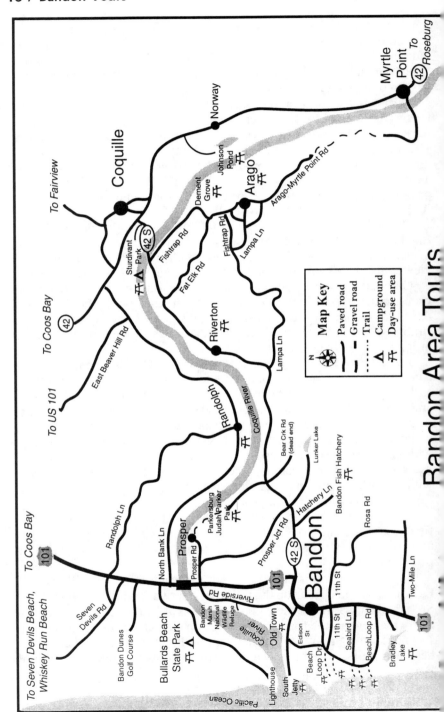

Bandon Area Tours

park beach accesses, including Face Rock. From that particular access you can study Face Rock, a low-lying rock a short distance out in the ocean. It's supposed to look like a face staring up from the sea, the visage of an Indian maiden trapped by a malevolent ocean spirit.

The road eventually loops back to US 101 at a point about 3 miles south of downtown Bandon. Turn left (N) to return to Bandon.

Bullards Beach State Park is Bandon's other popular beach. It's north of town, across the Coquille River Bridge along US 101. In addition to a state park campground that features rental yurts, there are many day-use areas, trails, a boat ramp, equestrian camp, and the Coquille River Lighthouse, which is open seasonally. Beachcoming is a favorite activity among Bandon visitors, and the beaches near the jetties sometimes have colorful rocks and the occasional agate. Storms sometimes shift the rocks to other beaches, such as those below Coquille Point along Beach Loop Drive.

Just north of Bullards Beach State Park along US 101 is the access road to Bandon Dunes, an upscale links-style golf course opened in the late 1990s and fast becoming one of the top-ranked courses in the nation. There are two 18-hole courses with fabulous views. The clubhouse features a restaurant and lounge, and there are overnight accommodations. Ambitous expansions are planned.

Bradley Lake: About 3.6 miles south of the stoplight at US 101 and 11st in Bandon is the access road to Bradley Lake. This small, freshwater lake has a day-use area and a boat ramp, and offers welcome respite on a windy summer day. Most of the shoreline is private property.

Once you've explored Bandon's beaches and parks, you might want to do a bit more exploring. Among the interesting nearby places is New River. See chapter 5 for details.

Another popular option is to head upriver on one of the roads that follows the Coquille River through peaceful countryside.

Upriver routes: The main route from Bandon and US 101 is Highway 42S, picturesque enough, but with lots of fast-driving local traffic. There are some nice country lanes to explore along the way, and even a little detour, and you connect with a back road that leads to Myrtle Point and other destinations.

North Bank Ln. is much mellower, and begins just north of the Coquille River Bridge, near Bullards Beach State Park. It meanders over to Highway 42, just north of Coquille. A logical loop is to drive up Highway 42S and return via North Bank Ln. Here are directions:

From US 101 in Bandon at the stoplight by Bandon Shopping Center, head east on Highway 42S, following signs to Coquille, 18 miles. The road heads past businesses and residences, as well as cemeteries dating to the white settlement of Bandon. In 0.5 mile is Hatchery Rd., leading to Bandon Fish Hatchery, always worth a look.

Continuing east, the road winds through forest and eventually drops into the coastal plain, although the Coquille River is about a mile north. 3 miles along is a crossroads, with signs indicating Parkersburg Rd. and Judah Park County Park to the left (N). The park is a couple of miles up the paved road. It's a small patch of slanting lawn under spreading myrtle trees on a slope across the road from the river, but alas, has no public access to the water itself.

Continuing east on 42S, you'll pass Lampa Mt. Ln. Information about the route is at the end of this section. Next along 42S is Riverton, where there's a boat ramp and picnic tables. This was another early-day settlements along the Coquille River, with a sawmill and other industries.

Follow 42S as it enters the Coquille River Valley, passing Fat Elk Rd. and crossing a raised causeway through pasturelands flooded in winter. The road swings up and over a bridge across the Coquille River. The city of Coquille's Sturdivant Park is on the other side, offering a boat ramp, day-use and camping in summer and early fall. There are foundation blocks and artifacts from an early-day sawmill, and a plaque honors the contributions of WWI's "Spuce Soldiers."

For details about Coquille, see chapter 14.

The road encounters Highway 42. To return to Bandon, turn left (N) and follow Highway 42 about 4 miles, then turn left (W) on North Bank Ln. This easy river road is almost guaranteed to lower your blood pressure. It lazes through countryside dotted with livestock and a few ranches and residences, and offers plenty of nice views of the valley and the river as it travels 18 miles back to US 101. Once at the highway, turn left (S) and cross the bridge over the Coquille River to return to Bandon.

Once across the bridge, turn right (W) on Riverside Drive. It skirts along the edge of Bandon Marsh National Wildlife Refuge, and there's an overlook and interpretive area along the way. Follow Riverside Drive to the waterfront area of Old Town.

Lampa Mt. Tour: This is another trek along the quiet back roads near Bandon. Because of intensive logging in recent years, it's not the prettiest tour in this book, but it's fun to wander along these little-traveled country roads. You can also use this route to connect to other back roads to Myrtle Point and other destinations.

From US 101 at the stoplight near Bandon Shopping Center, head east on Highway 42S, following signs to Coquille. See the previous section for details about this trek. In about 7 miles, turn right (S) on Lampa Mt. Ln., which heads through a narrow valley rimmed by recently-clearcut and replanted ("reprod") slopes. The fields are seasonally flooded, but come back green and vibrant in spring and early summer, to the contentment of cattle, horses, sheep, goats and other livestock.

There are some classic abandoned farmhouses and barns along this route. They slowly surrender to the elements, some seemingly kept standing only by solid thickets of blackberry vines.

The road loops up out of the valley and climbs a slope, going north for a bit before topping out and dropping down into a pocket valley. After about 5 miles the road encounters a "T" intersection. Lampa Ln. continues to the right (E), heading to Myrtle Point. For details about this route, see chapter 14. Continue straight ahead on what is now Fishtrap Rd. Views of the vast Coquille River Valley open up to the northeast, as the road skirts above the river and floodplain. In another mile is another junction, with the road to the right leading into the settlement of Arago.

Keep going north on what is now Fat Elk Rd. as it cuts through the middle of cattle ranches and passes a few country residences. The road takes on another bit of pretty forest again, then drops down into the river plain and meets Highway 42S. A right turn will take you to Highway 42 and Coquille in 3 miles; turn left to return to Bandon, 15 miles.

7. Singing Sands and Strange Shapes: The Oregon Dunes

Road conditions: *Paved, year-'round access. Some roads and trails subject to winter flooding.*

Notes: *Access from US 101 begins just north of North Bend/ Coos Bay Area, and continues about 40 miles to just north of Florence. Year-'round camping, day-use, hiking, horseback riding, OHV access, boating, swimming, fishing. Day-use fees for entry into all developed areas within Oregon Dunes National Recreation Area.*

Mention the Oregon Dunes and most people think about sand. Would you believe it's really about water? Starting with the ocean, of course, which continues to deliver and redistribute the sand. Then there's fresh water, falling in metric tons through winter and spring, coursing endlessly from coastal mountains, often impounded into lakes within sight and sound of the sea.

Flowing from the lakes are outlets to the sea, while underneath the sand is another vast river of fresh water, an aquifer routinely tapped by municipal water agencies throughout "dunes country."

You can't travel far in the dunes without encountering water, be it salt or "sweet" or a brackish mixture of the two. Vast areas of low-lying parts of the dunes are often flooded during the rainy season.

Still, the dunes are best known for dreamy reaches of sculpted sand, shifting by day and by season. The whole profile of the dunes actually changes throughout the year, thanks to prevailing weather patterns that have the wind arriving from the north in summer, and the south in winter. What was a sharply-sculpted ridge of brittle sand in February can

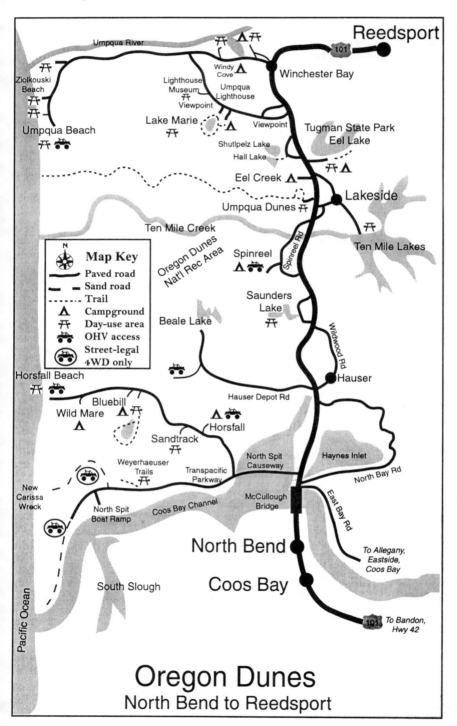

Oregon Dunes
North Bend to Reedsport

turn into a smoothly-contoured mound of powder in summertime. Wide-open stretches are becoming less common, though, with the intrusion of European beach grass, planted to stabilize embankments of coastal rivers, but now a nuisance.

What's more, beach grass growing close to the shore has another stabilizing effect; blocked by strands of grass, windblown sand falls to the ground, building up a foredune. The foredune creates what's called a deflation plain behind it, where -- protected from the wind -- beach grass, shrubs and trees gain a foothold.

The beach grass spreads inland, taking over more open sand every year. Efforts to remove it have included everything from fire to bulldozers to sprinkler systems that douse the grass with saltwater.

Scotch broom is another introduced species slowly creeping in everywhere. Its bright yellow blooms last into the summer, and it's almost as intrusive as the notorious, thorny gorse, which also produces a sunny yellow bloom in spring and summer.

Thanks to these invaders, the dunes are changing significantly. Aerial photos from the 1930s show 80 percent open sand, while today less than 20 percent remains. Indeed, without some drastic changes man-made or natural, the dunes will probably be grown over in 50 years.

Much remains unanswered about the Oregon Dunes. How and when were they formed? Just how much water is in the aquifer underneath, and can it be tapped indefinitely?

Researchers are puzzling these mysteries. The most popular theory in recent years has the sand's origin in the distant inland mountains of the Cascade Range. Rivers such as the Umpqua that flowed from the Cascades were thought to have brought down eroded rock and other material, which was then ground into sand by the ceaselessly churning ocean. The sand is brought to shore -- and taken back and forth again and again -- by wind and weather.

More recent research suggests the sand originated much closer to the ocean, eroding not from the Cascades but from coastal headlands and the Coast Range. While that theory is still being studied, it's been bolstered by recently findings that the Oregon Dunes are an exposed portion of a vast "dunes sheet" that underlies much of the West Coast.

Scientific debate notwithstanding, there's no doubt about the fact that to most folks, the Oregon Dunes are a vast playland. Some explore in off-road vehicles, while others wander by foot, horseback and sometimes sled-dog carts among the strange world of soft shapes and lights and textures.

You can find this world in every season, and every season is a discovery, whether you travel in off-road vehicle or on foot, or even by boat, canoe or kayak.

There are popular, well-marked access areas throughout the dunes, stretching 40 miles from Coos Bay to north of Florence.

The U.S. Forest Service manages this as the Oregon Dunes National Recreation Area, with headquarters in Reedsport; they have information and maps, as do local chambers. A $5 day-use fee is required for all areas, with seasonal passes and senior discounts available.

Driving in the dunes: Much of the dunes are open for off-highway vehicles (OHVs), as are a few stretches of beach. Most of the popular access points have adjacent campgrounds and rental facilities if you haven't brought along your own OHV.

From North Bend, head north on US 101, crossing the McCullough Bridge. About 0.5 mile north, turn left (W) on the North Spit Causeway, following the sign to Horsfall Beach and Oregon Dunes.

The road crosses the causeway, then a bridge, and passes a Weyerhaeuser paper mill. Cross railroad tracks and take the right fork, entering the Oregon Dunes National Recreation Area. (To the left is Transpacific Parkway, heading to a BLM boat launch in 3 miles. See chapter 2 for more information.) You'll encounter entry signs and a vending machine for day-use passes, and just beyond that, Horsfall campground, with direct sand access for OHVers.

The road continues past a day-use area officially called Sandtrack but known by generations of locals as Showoff Hill. Outfitted only with a piece of old cardboard on which to slide down, many a youthful daredevil has challenged this tall, smooth dune.

The road next encounters the parking area for Bluebill Lake Trail, then Bluebill Lake campground, a horse staging area, and several OHV access points. The road ends at Horsfall Beach, where there's an overflow campground and OHV access to sand dunes and the beach. The beach is open to vehicles for about 10 miles north, to Ten Mile Creek.

Back on US 101, 1.5 miles north of Horsfall Access is USFS Spinreel campground, with adjacent OHV staging area. The main route for OHVs heads west more or less following Ten Mile Creek to the sea, with many, many side tracks fanning out into the dunes.

The next OHV access is out of Winchester Bay; follow signs to the Umpqua Beach area and head to the end of the road at Ziolkouski Beach. The beach here is off-limits, but OHVs can explore many, many miles of inland dunes.

The next vehicle access is north of Gardiner. From Gardiner, continue north on US 101, climbing the hill past the International Paper plant, and in 2 miles turn left (W) on Sparrow Park Rd. Follow this gravel road 4 miles west to its terminus at the beach, which is open to vehicles south to the Umpqua River jetty and north to Takenitch Creek.

In the northern dunes around Florence, there are OHV access points along beaches and dunes at the Siltcoos River recreation area and from the south jetty area of the Siuslaw River.

Kayaker Ron Wardman glides across the lilypad-dappled surface of Beale Lake. Wardman is author of a guidebook on local paddling opportunities. See the back of this book for details.

Boating notes: You could spend a long time exploring the many lakes and streams in the Oregon Dunes. There are launch ramps for boats and undeveloped put-ins for canoes and kayaks throughout the system, too many to name here. A few favorites include Saunders Lake, 6 miles north of McCullough Bridge on US 101. Not officially part of the Oregon Dunes, there's a county boat ramp here, and two small lakes for exploring.

Two miles beyond on US 101 is the USFS Spinreel campground, which has a small, gravel boat ramp into Ten Mile Creek. If no fallen trees block the channel, you can boat upstream to Ten Mile Lakes. The creek seaward gets pretty shallow after a mile or so, suitable only for kayaks and canoes. The creek's flow is different in every season, and weather, wind and tides affect conditions near the ocean, so use caution.

Ten Mile Lakes, adjacent to Lakeside, about 10 miles north of the Coos Bay Area on US 101, are the first of many vast freshwater lakes surrounded by forests that give you the impression you're up in the mountains somewhere. As the name implies, there are two lakes, and they're connected by a short channel.

There's a county boat ramp and several private marinas in Lakeside, and it's a popular lake for waterskiers. Members of the Coos Bay Yacht

Club located on a cove of the south lake bring out small sailboats for colorful races. Much of the shoreline is privately owned, and many houses are accessible only by boat.

Eel Lake is next, and in contrast to nearby Ten Mile Lakes, has a 5 mph speed limit for boats, and no development on its shores or forested hillsides. The entrance is adjacent to William Tugman State Park, just north of Lakeside on US 101. This horseshoe-shaped lake has many inlets and coves to explore. There's lots of wildlife, including nesting osprey, so a quiet approach in canoe or kayak can be rewarding.

Not far north of Eel Lake is Clear Lake, which is off-limits since it's Reedsport's water supply. Next, in the vicinity of the Umpqua Lighthouse, is Lake Marie, a little lake for easy paddling.

Winchester Bay is a popular access to the Umpqua River and the ocean. There's a big marina with several boat ramps and all the usual services. A few miles beyond Winchester Bay is Reedsport, where there are more boat ramps providing access to the Umpqua River, its tributary Schoenfield Creek, and its neighbor, the Smith River.

North of Reedsport is Gardiner, where there's another Umpqua River boat ramp. Farther north along US 101 is Elbow Lake, with an unimproved launch site for small boats. Next is the vast Takenitch Lake, with a USFS boat ramp adjacent to a campground.

Carter Lake, a long, narrow body of water that parallels US 101, has a USFS boat launch.

Siltcoos Lake, largest in the Oregon Dunes, comes along next, with a boat ramp at Westlake/Dunes City. From this ramp, canoes and kayaks can paddle an officially designated "trail" down Siltcoos Creek to the ocean. A portage has been constructed to get paddlers around an impound dam about 2 miles downstream from the lake.

Continuing north on US 101, Honeyman State Park offers access to tiny Cleawox Lake and to Woahink Lake, deepest in the dunes. The town of Florence, with the Siuslaw River and several small lakes offering more boating opportunities, is just north of here.

Hiking in the dunes

Horsfall Beach: This is the sentimental local favorite for that long walk on the beach. Its flat expanse in either direction invites opportunity for significant strolling, whether for introspection, inspiration or deep conversation. This can also be the most popular -- *populated* -- beach in summer, and walkers must share the beach north of the parking area with vehicles. Walking north for 10 miles gets you to aptly-named Ten Mile Creek, and depending on weather, river flow and tide conditions, you can ford the creek and continue walking another 10 miles to the mouth of the Umpqua River near Winchester Bay.

At one time the main "road" for stagecoaches north to the Umpqua River, the beach was named for pioneer doctor William Horsfall, legendary for his efforts to care for settlers in Coos County's far-flung river and forest country. Once, being rowed across the bay to deliver a baby, the boat sank and he had to swim to shore carrying his medical bag in one hand above water.

Vehicles are prohibited south of Horsfall Beach. You can walk south to Coos Bay's north jetty, about 2 miles; about 1 mile along and just offshore is the wreck of the *New Carissa*.

To get to Horsfall Beach, follow directions in the previous section on driving in the dunes.

Bluebill Lake: On the road out to Horsfall Beach is Bluebill Lake Trail. Follow directions to Horsfall Beach in the section above on "Driving in the dunes." The trailhead is just before Bluebill campground, about 1.6 miles along Horsfall Road from the Oregon Dunes entrance. The 1-mile trail loops around the lake, with a boardwalk system over marshy sections at the south end. Once across the boardwalk, the footing gets a bit sandy and trail signs may not be in place. Watch for blue-banded posts that mark the way. At a "Y" junction, bear right on a trail that goes under tall trees. It will lead to the edge of the campground. The footpath crosses a wooden bridge at the north end of the lake and continues to an intersection with the trail you came in on.

Spinreel: About 8 miles north of McCullough Bridge on US 101 is USFS Spinreel campground, described previously in the vehicle and boating sections. There are a few sections of trail heading west from the OHV staging area along Ten Mile Creek, but side canyons keep forcing you back to the main sand road to the beach. *It's not safe to walk on Spinreel area roads or others used by dune buggies and OHVs.*

Umpqua Dunes: A much better walking experience is in the Umpqua Dunes area just north of Ten Mile Creek, in a section off-limits to motorized vehicles. Look for the USFS Umpqua Dunes Trail signs on the west side of US 101 about 0.2 mile north of the Lakeside exit.

Interpretive signs and a brochure offer more details. There's a 1-mile loop trail, or you can turn this into a classic dunes adventure, climbing one of the system's highest sand hills, or pressing on to the beach through one of its largest expanses of open sand.

The 1-mile loop trail offers a microcosm of the dunes environment. Many of the trees, plants and animals found throughout the 40-mile-long dunes system are in residence here, from the bonsai-looking shore pines to the towering wild rhododendrons to the intriguing mosses and lichens.

The longer trek takes more adventuresome hikers through some of the most dramatic landscapes in the Oregon Dunes, with tall sand ridges, wind-carved formations known as "yardangs," and a textbook example of a "tree island" surrounded by sand.

If you're going for the longer hike, a couple of words of caution. As noted earlier in this chapter, coastal winds generally come from the north in summer, and it's windy nearly every afternoon. Summer months are dry; the sand is softer and the going slower.

In winter, wind arrives from the south, usually accompanied by rain, not all of which soaks into the sand. Many places remain flooded well into summer. This is especially true in the deflation plain near the beach, and in particular along the far end of this trail! *Bring high-top rubber boots or other waterproof footwear.*

No matter what the season -- even in overcast weather -- sun against sand equals sunburn potential. I don't care if it's January or July, you've got to convince yourself and everyone who may be with you that unless you apply sunblock, you're going to get sunburned.

Equally important is to bring -- and drink -- water. As obvious as these last two topics may seem, they're often the most commonly-overlooked among dune trekkers.

Finally, caution youngsters against burrowing into the sides of dunes; tunnels can and do collapse with tragic consequences.

OK, let's go: From the parking area the trail heads across a footbridge and up along a slope protected on one side by a sturdy retaining wall. Leafy waxmyrtle trees and spiky shore pines provide the forest canopy. Oregon grape, salal, huckleberry and rhodies -- the latter of which bloom from late May to mid-June -- line the way, overshadowing some of the action closer to the ground.

That fluorescent-green stuff is reindeer lichen, so called because it resembles the fine fur growing on reindeer horns. Lichens are intriguing organisms that consist of algae living symbiotically with a fungus. Sometimes whimsically called a "fungus that's farming," lichen obtains its nourishment from the algae and, in turn, absorbs and retains the water needed by the algae for photosynthesis.

Up around the next bend is a "T" intersection, with a trail straight ahead to Eel Creek campground. Turn left, heading up another slope with a retaining wall protecting the trail. You'll top a rise and emerge onto sand, meeting the first blue-banded posts that mark this trail. A marshy expanse of sand, thick with a stubby stand of red fescue, lies to the south, and the trail skirts around a hillside of Oregon grape, salal and wind-sculpted shore pines.

The trail heads north through the woods. Before long open sand again, with a big dune just ahead. The trail -- look for the banded posts -- heads around the dune, but a hike to the top is worth the trudge. The view commands nearly the entire southern section of the Oregon Dunes, with the sea filling the western horizon.

Continuing the hike, align yourself with the blue-banded posts and walk west through the dunes. You might consider glancing back to note the location of water tanks in the hills to the east; you can use them as landmarks on your return in case you have difficulty locating the blue-banded posts or want to do a little "open dune" exploration.

The trail heads north of the tree island, passing over and along ob-

Eel Lake Trail in Tugman State Park

lique dunes, some with steep sandy slopes, others with softer-looking flanks. The shapes of the dunes change depending on the seasonal winds, thus the expression "living dunes."

Low areas hold pools of rainwater surrounded by beach grass, wildflowers, low-growing scrub and trees. Approach quietly and you might spot birds and other wildlife.

The sense of isolation out here can be delicious, and just when you wonder if you can go on, you clear the dunes and arrive at the deflation plain -- a forest of stubby pines and thick underbrush. The trail turns north for a bit before picking a way through the brush. As noted, parts of the trail are flooded nearly year-'round.

The sound of the surf will urge you on, and suddenly, over a short wooden footbridge, here's the beach.

To the south, the mouth of Ten Mile Creek is 2.5 miles; north it's about 8 miles to Umpqua River.

If you return the way you came, remember to stay north of the tree island and head for the water tanks on the hills.

Eel Lake Trail: Just north of Lakeside on US 101 is William Tugman State Park and Eel Lake. There's a campground, and a day-use area bounded by large expanses of lawn kept green and mowed all year. Here, too, is a handicapped-accessible fishing dock, boat ramp and group picnic area. There's also an excellent new hiking/mountain biking trail along a portion of the lakeshore, part of what's envisioned as a 30-mile trail that will eventually encircle the lake. As noted in the earlier section on boating, Eel Lake has no development along its shore or on the wooded hillsides above, and there's a speed limit on boats, so the setting is peaceful. This forested lake seems far removed from the world of the Oregon Dunes, yet such freshwater lakes and their outlets to the sea are very much a part of this unusual region.

The trail begins just south of the day-use area. To find the trailhead, follow a path along Eel Creek, the lake's outlet. Pass a concrete containment pond for fish, and continue south, watching to the left for a wooden footbridge over Eel Creek. The well-engineered trail follows the lake's many contours, weaving through a forest of fir, hemlock, spruce and cedar. Little footbridges cross seasonal streams, and there are overlooks with hand-hewn wooden benches. The vista points reveal increasingly tantalizing bits of this lake, which is deceptively large.

A quiet approach to the many coves and inlets usually results in some bird sightings. There are nesting osprey and a variety of waterfowl. The coniferous forest provides a home for pileated woodpecker, Pacific slope flycatcher, brown creeper, Wilson's warbler and band-tailed pigeon. Nighthawks have also been spotted, and bald eagles from nearby Ten Mile Lakes fly over to hunt for fish.

At this writing, the path ends about 4 miles along, so you'll have to backtrack out.

Hall/Shutlpelz Lake: This day-use area has trails leading to two nifty little lakes surrounded by Dunes-country forest and tall sand slopes. Hall Lake has several nice picnic spots along its shoreline. Along the creek that drains out of nearby Shutlpeltz Lake is a small waterfall. Listen for it near the north shore of Hall Lake and you can figure out which of the many little side trails leads to it.

You can also launch expeditions out into the open dunes. There are terrific views of the miles of ice-cream-scoop dunes, of several tree islands, and of the Pacific Ocean. The beach is about 3 miles away, but for the moment there's no way to get to it through the dense brush and tress of the deflation plain. You'd have to walk about 2 miles south to Umpqua Dunes Trail, which has a corridor through the brush. (Umpqua Dunes Trail is described earlier in this chapter.) As with that hike and others in the open sand, use caution in this part of the dunes. It's easy to get disoriented. Note landmarks that will help you find your way back!

Access to the Hall Lake area is via Wildwood Drive, across US 101 from the entrance to Tugman State Park. Follow Wildwood Drive north about 0.5 mile to roadside parking, and watch for small USFS signs at trails leading to the lakes. The Forest Service plans improvements which may be completed by the time you visit.

Lake Marie: This little lake in the forests below Umpqua Lighthouse has a 1-mile perimeter trail through a picture-perfect mixed-species forest. Part of the path tunnels through huge wild rhodies, and there's a side path at the lake's south end that leads to open dunes. Follow signs from US 101 to Umpqua Lighthouse, and look for Lake Marie just beyond the state park campground.

Umpqua Beach/Ziolkouski Beach: The Umpqua River meets the sea at Winchester Bay, about 23 miles north of the Coos Bay Area. The town of Winchester Bay offers shops, restaurants, motels, other services, and there's a commercial and sport fishing harbor, with fishing piers, boat launch's, campgrounds, RV parks and OHV rental places.

The beach begins at Umpqua River's south jetty, with an unusual rock triangle built into it to deflect waves. For an overview of the jetty and surrounding dunes, check out the Umpqua Lighthouse area; follow signs west from Winchester Bay. The light is open for tours and there's an adjacent visitors' center in a former Coast Guard building.

To get to the beach, continue on the road along the river's edge. The first beach access is a county park, popular with surfers who like to challenge waves alongside the jetty. It's also one of the few free accesses to the beach hereabouts.

The next two beach accesses are part of the Oregon Dunes NRA, so fees are required to enter. No matter where you choose to access this beach, called alternately Umpqua Beach and Ziolkouski Beach, you'll find a vehicle-free strand from the south jetty 10 miles southward.

At road's end are restrooms, a group picnic area with covered pavilion, and OHV access. OHV rentals have been available here in recent years, although as noted vehicles must stay off the beach. To the southeast is another of the dunes system's nine "tree islands," a remnant of forest completely surrounded by sand.

There are other hiking opportunities farther north in the Oregon Dunes, including the Three Mile Lake Trail off Sparrow Park Road north of Gardiner, an excellent trail system near Takenitch Lake, a trail below the Oregon Dunes Overlook, the Taylor Dunes Trail near Carter Lake, a hiker/mountain bike trail at Siltcoos Lake and a number of other trails in the Siltcoos Recreation Area.

But what's that *sound?*

Another curiosity of the Oregon Dunes is what some describe as their "singing." A high-pitched noise seems to emanate from the dunes at times, not necessarily related to wind, weather or the sounds of the ocean. People have called it singing and squeaking, while others say it sounds like the playing of violins.

The phenomenon is apparently not confined to the Oregon Dunes. Much has been written about sound vibrations in open dunes during certain times of wind and silence.

Such accounts span the globe from Australia to Denmark to Long Island, New York. Charles Darwin noted a "chirping noise" on the "fine siliceous sands" leaving Socego, and he pursued a Middle Eastern legend of a monastery bell long buried in sand that was still heard to ring.

In his 1858 book *The Cruise of the Betsy*, anthropologist Hugh Miller wrote about sands that produced a "shrill sonorous note, resembling that produced by a waxed thread when tightened between teeth and a hand, then tripped by a tip of the forefinger." Henry Thoreau heard singing sounds while hiking in dunes of New Hampshire, saying the sound resembled that made by a "finger rubbing across wet glass."

Current theories take on a more scientific tone, speculating that layers -- or even particles -- of sand are coated with different densities of salt, thus vibrating at different ranges when blown or rubbed against each other. Layers and particles could also be reacting in different ways to wetting and evaporation, a process that creates "cushions" between layers which then grind against each other with eerie, audible effects.

Still, it's transfixing in its way, like watching gravity and the wind suddenly create a silent, spreading "sandfall" in the side of a dune. In other words, it's just sand in motion, rolling downhill. Singing!

8. Above the Blue: Catching Slough to Blue Ridge

Road conditions: *Paved except for 5 miles. Year-'round access.*
Notes: *30-mile roundtrip from Coos Bay. Access to BLM Blue Ridge trail system, 12 miles of mountain bike/equestrian/OHV trails.*

Here's an easy jaunt from Coos Bay, out along the meanders of picturesque Catching Slough and up to the soaring panoramas of Blue Ridge. This prominent north-south ridge is visible to the southeast from many parts of the Coos Bay Area.

The forested slopes of Blue Ridge have yielded a bounty of timber for generations of loggers, and logging continues to this day. At its foot is Catching Slough, a main thoroughfare in the era when waterways served as part of the transportation network. Early-day travelers from Coos Bay took a ferry or boat to the end of Catching Slough, where the Wagon Road to Roseburg began.

These days, you can drive on levee roads above Catching Slough, intercept the Wagon Road for a look, then loop back on Blue Ridge. A nice outing if you have only a few hours to spare.

That said, among potential diversions along the way is the Blue Ridge trail system, 12 miles of old roads and new trails through peaceful woods.

Old tractor in honorable retirement out along Catching Slough

Getting There

At the "Y" on US 101 at the south end of Coos Bay, follow signs to Allegany, Coos River. The road crosses a bridge over railroad tracks, then a bridge over Isthmus Slough. Bear left (N) just across the bridge, following signs to Allegany.

You're passing through Eastside, once a separate town but now a district of Coos Bay. To the west across the channel is a Georgia-Pacific sawmill, sometimes with ships taking on lumber or wood chips. A tugboat fleet also calls this part of the waterway home base.

The road comes to a "T" intersection. Turn right (E), on Coos River Rd, following signs to Allegany, Catching Slough, Golden and Silver Falls State Park.

The road leaves the residential district, offering views north that take in the bay and McCullough Bridge.

Just past city limits are Southern Oregon Marine shipyards, busy with manufacturing and repairs of various types of vessels. The road crosses a high concrete bridge over Catching Slough, offering views of the upper reaches of the Coos Bay estuary.

Immediately across the bridge turn right (S) on East Catching Slough Rd. (For trips up Coos River, see chapters 9 and 10.)

You might think the name Catching Slough has something to do with catching fish, but it's actually named after an early settler. As noted earlier, this was a vital waterway in earlier days, but movement of people, goods and logs was very much dependant on the tides. Travelers headed up the channel tried to wait for an incoming tide to make the trip easier, while those headed down liked to go on an outgoing flow. The biggest

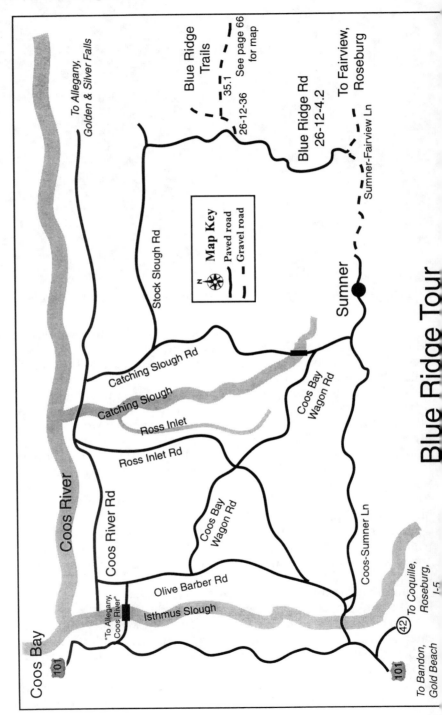

Blue Ridge Tour

challenge was not to get stuck in the mud on an outgoing tide.

Depending on the time of your visit, you'll see why. At low tide, a small channel is surrounded by mudflats. If you're here around high tide, the water brims to the banks.

If it's sunny, the waterway is a shimmering path through levees and marshes. A few small boat docks are all that remain of the once-vital river traffic, and old pilings sprout tufts of hardy grasses as they decay into the mudflats.

Classic weathered barns, still in use, seem right out of a calendar picture. About 4 miles out is another relic: a weathered sawmill perched on pilings, slowly collapsing into the slough. In the building nearest the road you can spot a big, rusty headrig saw.

About 6 miles out Catching Slough Rd. (7 miles from Eastside) is a "Y" in the road. Follow the signs to Sumner; bearing right across a small bridge, then left. We're on the Coos Bay Wagon Road now. In 0.5 mile is a four-way stop. Turn left (E) on Fairview-Sumner Ln. and you'll roll into Sumner.

Sumner was a terminus of the Coos Bay Wagon Road when it was completed in 1872. The road was eventually extended into town, but in the early days this was where the harrowing experience began, or mercifully ended. Although only 58 miles, the trip through the rugged Coast Range sometimes took as long as *three days* to complete! (For a trip on Wagon Road, see chapter 13.)

The Sumner store is the lone vestige of commerce here, last chance for supplies on this trek.

The road rolls up through the valley. About 1 mile from Sumner pavement turns to gravel for a rugged uphill pull through thickly forested canyon. Imagine yourself in pioneer days traversing this trail, up and up through the huge trees and gigantic swordferns . . . no wonder travelers were so relieved to arrive in the open space of a valley!

2 miles out of Sumner is a paved road heading uphill, to the left (N). Signs if in place identify this as BLM 26-12-4.2 and Blue Ridge Lookout Rd. There may also be a sign pointing the way to the Blue Ridge trails system.

However, the most important identifying feature is the blacktop pavement. It's the only paved road you'll pass on this stretch, so don't feel hesitant about taking an "unmarked" route if signs are missing.

By the same token, there are many logging spurs along Blue Ridge Rd., but only one paved road, and by sticking to it, you can't get lost!

And speaking of paved road, this sure is a nice one in places. It's more like a landscaped driveway through the woods! But as always, be alert for log trucks year-'round and hunters in autumn.

The forest is under standard management pattern, from groves of 60-year-old trees to slopes recently replanted to patches still smoldering with slash burns.

On this first stretch, the road ascends groves of mixed forest -- fir, hemlock, spruce, cedar, alder -- with a few impressive specimens. If you're feeling adventurous, explore a side road or two, but don't wander too far without a map or a good sense of direction. The woods and roads start to look the same around every turn!

In addition to providing a wealth of timber, Blue Ridge also had rock quarries, with seams of hard igneous rock used in building rocks and jetties.

There once was a fire lookout tower up here, but it's long gone. A power line along the road feeds a microwave facility. About 3 miles along the ridgeline road is a "Y." To continue this driving tour, take the left fork, sticking on pavement.

At this intersection are gravel roads that lead to the BLM Blue Ridge trail system. (Details at the end of this chapter.)

The road immediately begins to descend, and in less than 1 mile is a suddenly-emerging vista that opens north onto views of Coos Bay and beyond, to sand dune and sea.

The view is particularly inspiring in clear weather. Immediately below is the Catching Slough country traversed earlier. You'll have fun getting your bearings, then slowly picking out such landmarks as McCullough Bridge.

And yes, take a good look out to sea. Find a low point in the hills and study the water . . . that's right, those are foamy tops of waves breaking on the shore . . . all the way from here, how about that!

This stop is the high point of the tour, and since there aren't any official facilities along the way, it's the best impromptu picnic spot.

When you're ready to continue, stick to the ridgeline road as it trends northward, and before long you'll encounter a few homes. The road comes to a "T" intersection at Stock Slough Rd, a paved county road. Turn left (W), downhill.

Houses and ranches hug the slopes, and in 2 miles Stock Slough Rd. ends, at Catching Slough Rd. This terrain should look familiar, since you passed it on the way out. Turn right (N) on Catching Slough Rd. and follow it back the way you came, back to town.

Blue Ridge Trail System: Open to off-highway vehicles (OHVs), mountain bicyclists, equestrians and hikers, this 12-mile system utilizes existing spur roads and several miles of new trails to form loops through middle-growth forest managed by the BLM atop Blue Ridge. The trails dip up and down through corridors of Oregon grape, salal, huckleberry and rhododendrons, the latter blooming with glad effect in late May and early June. There aren't any raging rivers or spectacular waterfalls or even any big views along the trails, but there's a palpable stillness in the woods up here. It's a peaceful place.

It can also be confusing, however, since trail signs are frequently missing. The BLM uses brown "Carsonite" milepost-like signs to point the way, but they disappear fast. You can obtain a map from local bike shops and the BLM office, or from their web site. Or use this book!

You can explore the place by vehicle and choose a trailhead from which to stage an expedition. Once on the trails, best advise it to follow the ruts of previous riders. The trails often cross or travel on vehicle roads, which are better marked -- helpful if you lose your bearings.

Also note that some trails are one-way only.

To get to the trails, refer to the previous section, traveling along Blue Ridge Rd., BLM 26-12-4.2 to the intersection with BLM 35.0. Signs if intact point the way to Blue Ridge Trails.

Turn right (NE) on 35.0 and in a few hundred feet turn right (E) on 35.1. The road dips down past a water storage pond, then goes uphill. It becomes a forest lane between stands of trees, with a powerline running alongside the road. About 0.5 mile along are trail crossings. At a "T" intersection, turn left (N) on 35.4 and in less than 1 mile you'll pass two trail crossings: potential staging areas. You can make a vehicle loop by continuing on 35.4 and turning left (W) on 25.1. Follow it to 35.0 and turn left (S) to return to the main Blue Ridge Rd.

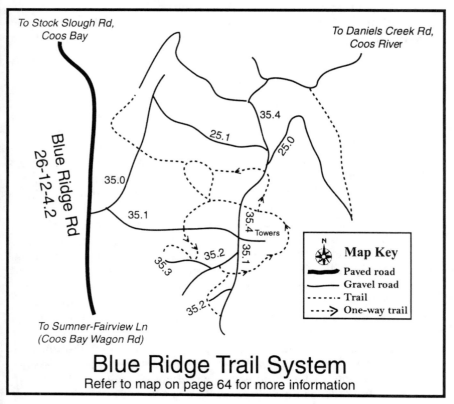

Blue Ridge Trail System
Refer to map on page 64 for more information

9. Golden and Silver Falls State Park/"Round the Bay

Road conditions: *Paved except for last 5 miles. Year-'round access.*

Notes: *50-mile roundtrip from Coos Bay. Camping, day-use, boating, fishing, swimming.*

Golden and Silver Falls State Park, about 25 miles east of the Coos Bay Area, offers two waterfalls set amidst 157 acres of forest spared from early-day forest fires and logging. A highlight is a walk along a trail "above the falls" on an old road hewn from solid rock.

Getting to the falls involves a drive along the picturesque river country of the Coos Bay Area, with a handful of picnic areas, boat ramps and campgrounds along the way. The falls are the second most-popular scenic attraction in the area, sometimes crowded with visitors in summer, but this trip works in every season.

In summer, for example, the weather can be cold and foggy (or windy!) in town while upriver it's a nice summer day. You can sit right under lacy Silver Falls for a refreshing shower.

Don't try that in winter or spring, though, when the falls are roaring full blast! Sunny interludes in springtime bring out the wild rhododendrons and other flowers, adding to the show. In autumn, the leafy trees of river country blaze with color.

Outfit yourself depending on the season; in summer bring swim gear, sunblock and bug repellant. In winter and spring, waterproof footwear for walking on the trails.

Getting There

The way to Golden and Silver Falls State Park is well marked. At the "Y" at the south end of Coos Bay on US 101, follow signs to Coos River, Allegany. The road crosses a bridge over railroad tracks, then goes over Isthmus Slough Bridge.

As you cross the bridge, you can see a couple of the Coos Bay Area's last operating sawmills. Upstream, to the right, is the Coastal Fibre Co. mill, with stacks of logs awaiting processing. To the left is a sprawling sawmill operation that was once home to the Coos Bay Lumber Co. It was the largest sawmill in the west, built to handle old-growth trees. Georgia-Pacific took over in later years, removing most of the old buildings, and now has a compact, highly automated operation to process smaller logs, which you'll see stacked around the site.

Bear left after crossing the bridge. The road skirts along the slough, directly across from the GP mill. You might spot ships or barges along the wharf taking on logs, lumber or wood chips. Closer at hand are docks for one of Coos Bay's tugboat fleets.

You're passing through Eastside here, once a separate town, now

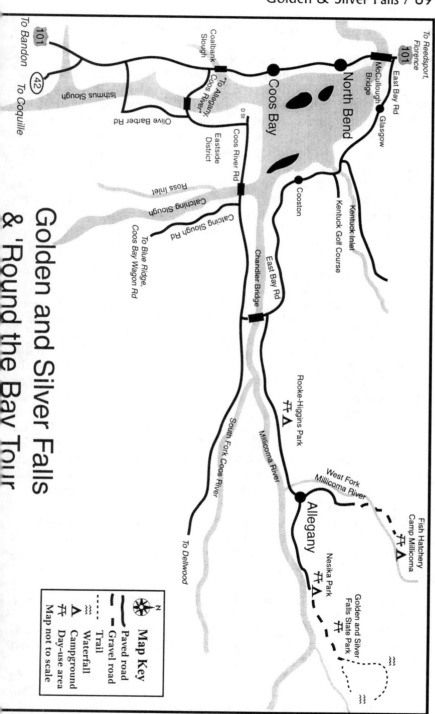

Golden and Silver Falls
& 'Round the Bay Tour

To Reedsport,
Florence

To Bandon

To Coquille

101
42

Coalbank
Slough

Isthmus Slough

Olive Barber Rd

To Allegany,
Coos River

D St

Eastside
District

Coos River Rd

McCullough
Bridge

East Bay Rd

Glasgow

Coos Bay

North Bend

Kentuck Inlet

Kentuck Golf Course

Cooston

Ross Inlet

Catching Slough

Catching Slough Rd

To Blue Ridge,
Coos Bay Wagon Rd

Chandler Bridge

East Bay Rd

South Fork Coos River

Millicoma River

Rooke-Higgins Park

West Fork
Millicoma River

Allegany

Nesika Park

Fish Hatchery
Camp Millicoma

Golden and Silver
Falls State Park

To Dellwood

Map Key

N

Paved road
Gravel road
Trail
Waterfall
Campground
Day-use area
Map not to scale

consolidated with Coos Bay. The road comes to a "T" intersection. Turn right (E) on Coos River Rd., following signs to Allegany, Catching Slough, Golden and Silver Falls State Park.

The route winds around the residential district, with bay views opening up to the left. Next are the bustling Southern Oregon Marine (SOMAR) shipyards, where ocean-going barges are fabricated.

The road goes up and over a concrete bridge, which offers a brief, commanding view. Below is Catching Slough, another arm of the bay. If it's low tide, exposed mudflats testify to the sea's influence even at this far reach. (For an excursion out Catching Slough, chapter 8.)

Once across Catching Slough, the road drops onto a levee. This is still very much a tidal estuary, mostly seawater that flushes in and out twice daily. However, as might be deduced from the name, Coos River is the main tributary feeding the Coos Bay estuary, and along with adjacent Millicoma River was an important thoroughfare in the days before roads.

Tens of thousands of logs floated down the rivers to mills around the bay, and a fleet of boats ferried passengers, livestock and farm goods on a daily basis. Today the only boats you'll see carry anglers going after salmon, sturgeon, striped bass or shad. Old pilings along the riverbanks are the last remnant of the logging era. Rafts of cut trees were lashed to them as boatmen waited for outgoing tides to help move the logs to mills.

Just ahead is the green steel span of Chandler Bridge. Cross the bridge, following signs to Allegany. Bear right (E) once across the bridge. The road's on the north bank now, on a levee protecting pasturelands and homesteads.

The Coos River meets the Millicoma River, although the confluence isn't visible from this road. The Coos River heads southeast; we'll follow the Millicoma. About 4 miles up from Eastside is Doris Place boat ramp. The road twists through more farmland -- right through the middle of a few cattle ranches -- as it works upriver. You'll catch glimpses of the river, lined by big, leafy maples and myrtlewood trees.

Next landmark is Rooke-Higgins County Park, offering camping, picnicking and a boat launch. There are picnic tables with nice views of the river and surrounding farmlands. In autumn when the salmon are running, you might see a big coho leaping out of the water, or watch an angler land a fish.

About 2 miles beyond is the Riverside Tavern, once a popular stop for Sunday excursion boats on the river.

The road curves along the still-navigable river, past more pastures and scattered homesteads, finally curving around in front of the former Allegany School, now a post office and community building.

Around another turn is Allegany. The grocery store is a remnant of a community which boasted a sawmill and other businesses. On a hill across from the store are old church buildings and a schoolhouse.

The settlement was supposedly named by a settler from Allegheny County, Penn., who either didn't know how to spell it or wanted to distinguish this Allegany from others in Pennsylvania, Virginia, the Carolinas and California. At any rate, the word means "beautiful river" in the Seneca Indian language, so it's a fitting name.

The river splits again here. Continue ahead, following signs to Golden and Silver Falls State Park, 10 miles.

If Allegany is beautiful river, what's Millicoma? The origin is unclear; historians think it's a reference to the local Miluk tribe.

These days, property along the river remains in private hands, while the forested hills are pretty much divided between government and corporate timberlands. To the northeast is 92,000-acre Elliott State Forest, logged and tree-farmed to help fund public schools. You'll pass a road leading into it about 1 mile past Allegany at Marlow Creek. (For an excursion on this road, see chapter 10.)

Just past Marlow Creek is an entrance to Weyerhaeuser's Millicoma Tree Farm. Take the left fork, following signs to Golden and Silver Falls. The roads parallel each other for a bit.

How Weyerhaeuser ended up with this 210,000-acre tract of prime timberland is a fascinating story of 19th-century collusion and robber-baron shenanigans that ended with at least one player doing prison time. It started with a trade for private land given up in Washington State to create Mt. Rainier National Park. The company added to its holdings through the years, and continues active logging and reforestation. Weyerhaeuser allows limited access to the Millicoma Tree Farm during the fall deer hunting season, but the property is mostly closed the rest of the year.

In 4 miles is Nesika County Park, offering both a day-use area and a campground. Just before the day-use area is a popular swimming hole often complete with rope swing. The campground is a couple of turns beyond the day-use area. Both offer a nice place to stop and stretch, and breathe in the natural incense of big myrtlewood trees here. In fact, this is an official Myrtlewood Tree Corridor, and it's easy to see -- and smell -- why. They arch magnificently over the road, and fill the air with their distinctive scent.

Myrtlewood, also called California laurel, is highly prized in the region as an excellent hardwood for carving. You'll hear claims that it grows only in southern Oregon and the Holy Land, but it's actually found from here all the way to Baja California. As for the myrtlewoods of the Holy Land, they're a different (although related) tree.

The road turns to gravel not far from Nesika, eventually becoming one lane. The trees get bigger, the canyon gets narrower. The road hugs a hillside of swordferns as the river rushes through a cataract of huge boulders. And then you're in Golden and Silver Falls State Park.

Along with the two distinctive waterfalls, this 157-acre park holds

Silver Falls in all its mid-winter glory

remnants of old-growth forest that once covered the region.

There are three trail choices from the parking lot. Alas, trail signs are often missing due to theft and vandalism. At any rate, directly to the north is the trail to Silver Falls, a 10-minute hike. The trail follows an old road (about which more in a moment) along the west bank of Silver Creek, up through a canyon of towering trees. The trees grow furry with moss as you get closer to the falls, and the mountainsides are thick with swordferns. In winter and spring, Silver Falls is in full thunder, sending off a rainbow-laden mist. The flow is dramatically reduced in summer and fall, and it's often possible to sit directly beneath the cascade.

No matter what the season, the water is a mesmerizing curtain, soothing on a summer day, silky even in a storm.

A sign sometimes intact at the viewpoint says the Hillside Trail is closed, but it's possible to scramble around and over downed trees, boulders and wash-outs, to the base of Silver Falls. In low water times you can make your way to the trail on the other side of the falls, which leads back down to the parking area, or up to Golden Falls.

Golden Falls: Go east from the parking area across the footbridge. The trails split just across the bridge. Directly ahead to the east is a level, 10-minute stroll through grand old myrtlewoods to the foot of the falls. Go this way first, to give yourself inspiration for the hike to the top.

The 377-foot falls were named in 1880 after Coos Bay physician Charles Golden. The sheer rock walls offer a look at an exposed section of the siltstone Tyee Formation that underlies the region.

For the longer hike to the top of the falls, take the left (N) fork trail just across the footbridge from the parking area. The path heads immediately up the canyon slopes, through towering old forest. In about 5 minutes you'll come to Silver Falls. The trail continues on a switchback, above the route you've just ascended.

Note the width of this trail: just wide enough for a single old-time vehicle. This was in fact once a main road, blasted out of the mountainside in places, over which came oxen teams, old Model Ts, even log trucks!

The trail cuts along siltstone cliffs that ooze water through a thick coat of moss. Pass through a cleft of rock as big as two houses. Hear that roaring from the gorge? It gets louder with each step . . .

Now comes the famous stretch that was cleared with dynamite, then suddenly you're right alongside the falls!

Lone trees jut dramatically over the void, and flat rocks offer perches from which to contemplate the grandeur.

The pioneers who made this road used it to get through the woods to Loon Lake, and from there down to the Umpqua River and inland valleys. This final harrowing stretch at the top was completed in 1901 by men who hung from ropes and bored six-foot holes into the cliffs to set their charges.

An early photo shows an eight-horse team pulling an iron boiler over this road, and an auto stage line ran along here from 1912 to 1916. There were homesteads in the Upper Glenn Creek Valley from the late 1800s to the 1950s, as well as a Civilian Conservation Corps camp and state prison work camp. It wasn't unusual for logging trucks to make a couple of trips a day over this dizzying route!

In our era, there's not much to see if you keep following the trail to the east. The park boundary ends at private land logged and replanted in recent years. Still, old-timers fondly remember this area "above the falls", and there's a sense of isolation to this day.

When you're ready to come down, retrace your footfalls to the parking area. (In case you're wondering, the original logging road once crossed a bridge at the base of Silver Falls, and continued down the west side of the creek. That's why the trail doesn't seem so wide once you switchback down at the base of Silver Falls.)

Once back in the parking area, retrace your vehicle route, following signs to Coos Bay, 24 miles.

West Fork Millicoma River Tour: For an interesting detour on this route, you can go up West Fork Millicoma River Rd., which begins directly across from Allegany store. The paved road follows the lovely West Fork, turning to gravel in about 5.4 miles. It negotiates some rough uphill sections as it makes its way about 3 more miles to a former scout camp now available for camping, and to adjacent Daniels Creek fish hatchery, open to the public. There are also many places to access the river for fishing, but please respect private property signs. The river is popular in winter steelhead season, with some anglers launching drift boats. High-water times of winter and early spring also find kayakers challenging the rapids.

'Round the Bay Tour: A drive around the bay can be an enjoyable outing, with a close-up look at the fringes of the Coos Bay estuary, along with picturesque vistas of the bayside towns and McCullough Bridge. Start at either end of East Bay Rd; from the north end, just north of McCullough Bridge, or from Coos River near the green-steel span of Chandler Bridge.

The road passes through the small communities of Cooston and Glasgow, and wends past Kentuck Golf Course.

Getting There: For this excursion, we'll start at the south end, since it's along the tour to Golden and Silver Falls described earlier in this chapter. From the south end of Coos Bay along US 101, go left (SE) at the "Y" intersection, following signs to Coos River, Allegany. Follow the road across Isthmus Slough Bridge, and go left (N), still following Allegany and Coos River signs. In about 0.5 at a "T" intersection turn right (E) on Coos River Rd. After twisting through a residential area, the road crosses Catching Slough Bridge and continues upriver.

Follow the river road 2.3 miles to Chandler Bridge, and cross it. Once over the bridge and around a bend, turn left (N) on East Bay Rd. The road drops through a forest to the edge of the bay. Levees cut through marshy backwaters of the bay to form a few pastures for cattle, while mudflats hold driftwood and storm-tossed logs.

The wetlands actually perform a valuable engineering purpose here, protecting this side of the bay's uplands by absorbing the constant surge of water, winds, tides and storm-driven flotsam. There are a few unofficial places to stop along the road if you want to explore the tidal flats.

The road finds its way to the settlement of Cooston, then curves around and follows the margins of the bay to Kentuck Inlet. There's a golf course here, and a dead-end side road that wanders up Kentuck Inlet.

East Bay Rd. heads uphill, weaving above the bay through forest, with views of the glittering water and McCullough Bridge revealed around every turn. And soon you'll be in Glasgow, where a smattering of houses cluster on benchlands and hills. Around a few more turns is US 101. A left (S) turn takes you immediately over McCullough Bridge for a return to North Bend and Coos Bay.

10. The 1000/Marlow Creek Rd - Allegany to Loon Lake

Road conditions: *Paved and gravel.*
Notes: *About 90-mile loop from Coos Bay.* **Watch for log trucks.** *Best in late spring, during rhodie bloom, and in early autumn. Roads are muddy in winter, dusty in summer. Camping, day-use, fishing, boating, swimming. (Loon Lake; see also chapter 12.)*

This tour follows parts of a pioneer-era route from the Coos Bay region, and gives you a sense of what was involved in early-day travel. It passes through Allegany, discussed in the previous chapter, and eventually reaches Loon Lake, a pleasant little lake in the forests of the Coast Range.

Early-day routes to and from Coos Bay used the waterways to get as far inland as possible, then took paths along river canyons and over watershed divides. One of the earliest routes led up the Coos and Millicoma rivers, into the forested reaches of the Coast Range to Loon Lake, and from there down to Umpqua River where roads led inland to the Umpqua and Willamette valleys.

The heart of the journey is on gravel roads through the Elliott State Forest, an active logging tract that generates revenue for Oregon schools. Most of this territory was devastated by an 1868 wildfire, and grew back naturally. Harvesting began in earnest in the late 1950s, and continues to this day. Cutover areas are replanted and there are stands of old timber left intact for wildlife habitat and other concerns. The first part of what is now a 92,000-acre state forest was set aside in 1929, and named for state forester Francis Elliott, who did much of the work consolidating state-owned forest holdings around Oregon.

As mentioned, logging in the Elliott State Forest continues apace so watch out for trucks and equipment. As in coming at you head-on around the next sharp turn. You may also see active "shows" in operation, with men and equipment bringing in logs and loading them onto trucks.

The route will take you along some soaring ridgelines, with a seemingly endless sea of trees in every direction. Early summer brings wildflowers and wild rhodies, while in fall big leafy maples put on a colorful show in the canyons.

A highlight is Silver Creek Heritage Grove, a protected stand of old trees. Once through the forest, the route passes Loon Lake, with limited services and camping, swimming, boating and fishing. The return is via Highway 38 to Reedsport, then back to the Coos Bay Area on US 101.

Getting There

Refer to the previous chapter for directions to Allegany. There's a general store, last chance for supplies for many miles. Continue past the store and in less than 1 mile, turn left (N) on Marlow Creek Rd., also marked with a "1000" sign. Note your odometer reading or zero out your trip odometer here.

The name Marlow came from an Indian chief who lived here, and a remnant of native encampments along the creek is a midden of shells and debris. In later years, a logging railroad ran 7 miles up this canyon.

The road weaves through a mass of blackberries and passes a few homesteads, then turns to gravel as it encounters an interpretive sign at 0.3 mile. An Elliott State Forest sign is 1 mile up, and just past that, a three-forked intersection: bear right.

The road works steadily up the canyon, with the creek bubbling by and big alders and maples spreading a leafy roof. Thick with moss, the trees support tiny ferns sprouting high above the tangled forest floor.

Still climbing gradually, you'll pass mileposts and note the mass of Elk Ridge looming up ahead. Then suddenly, we're *really* climbing!

After negotiating some mean switchbacks, the road eases up a bit, with views opening to the west. You'll pass a turnout, then a waterhole for tanker trucks at 6.5 miles and an intersection with the 1370 Rd. Now the views really widen.

At 7.9 miles at the intersection with the 1400 Rd., bear right, following the 1000 Rd.

The access road to the Heritage Grove comes up next, at 8 miles, near a big gravel pile. To visit the grove, turn right (S) on Rd. 1440 (also marked 1430). Follow the road down and go right at the "Y" to the Silver Creek Heritage Grove, a 50-acre stand of 220-year old Douglas fir and hemlock.

The trees here were spared during the devastating fire of 1868, and eluded harvest by timber companies and the state after that. Jerry Phillips,

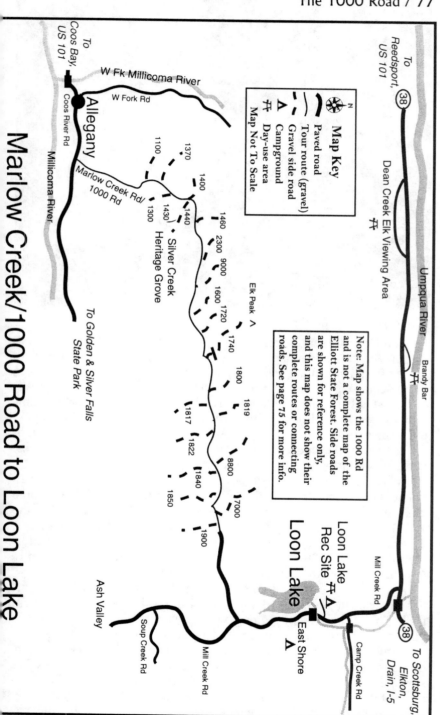

Marlow Creek/1000 Road to Loon Lake

Map Key

- 🧭 N
- Paved road
- Tour route (gravel)
- Gravel side road
- ▲ Campground
- 🏕 Day-use area
- Map Not To Scale

Note: Map shows the 1000 Rd and is not a complete map of the Elliott State Forest. Side roads are shown for reference only, and this map does not show their complete routes or connecting roads. See page 75 for more info.

To Reedsport, US 101
38

Dean Creek Elk Viewing Area

Umpqua River

Brandy Bar

Mill Creek Rd

Loon Lake Rec Site

Loon Lake

East Shore

Camp Creek Rd

38

To Scottsburg, Elkton, Drain, I-5

To Coos Bay, US 101

Coos River Rd

W Fk Millicoma River

W Fork Rd

Allegany

Millicoma River

Marlow Creek Rd/ 1000 Rd

1100

1370

1400

1300

1430

1440

1460

2300

9000

1600

1720

1740

1800

1819

1817

1822

8800

1840

7000

1850

1900

Silver Creek Heritage Grove

Elk Peak ▲

To Golden & Silver Falls State Park

Ash Valley

Soup Creek Rd

Mill Creek Rd

Curious residents always ready to greet visitors

Oregon Department of Forestry supervisor of the Elliott State Forest, recognized the stand as a potential preserve, and ensured the trees were spared from harvest. He oversaw acquisition of some equally old trees on adjacent Weyerhaeuser land, adding to the size of the heritage grove.

The stately firs are a tantalizing reminder of the grandeur once common to the region. Barring forest fire or a change in ODF philosophy, the trees may continue to grow. As the interpretive sign at the sight explains, they'll eventually give way to a forest dominated by hemlocks, in the natural progression of Coast Range forest.

Which is quite unlike the tree-farm appearance you'll return to when you make your way back to the 1000 Rd. and turn right (E) to continue this tour. You'll pass an intersection with the 1460 Rd. Bear right on the 1000 Rd., now descending through ferny hillsides of moderate-sized trees.

Keep passing many side roads and at 10 miles, at a big curving intersection with the 9000 Rd., bear right following the 1000 Rd. Now you're cruising the ridges, past more side roads marked and unmarked.

At about 14 miles is Rd. 1720, Elk Peak Rd., to the left. It's gated off to vehicles, but you can park in a turnoff and walk up to this prominent peak. There's been some logging, which opens up the view; you can see parts of the Umpqua region to the east, and a long way south and west.

Continuing on the 1000 Rd., head around the flanks of Elk Peak, up, down and up again. You'll pass many side roads for next few miles, but stick to 1000. More rolling ridges; in one stretch wild rhodies line both sides of the road, and there's some fine tall timber. Azaleas bloom, too, as the road descends, past clearcuts and regrowing slopes and alders.

A few challenging turns and at about 21 miles you'll encounter signs of civilization -- pavement! Cross a concrete bridge and proceed to a "T" intersection. Turn left (N) and in a moment you'll come to Loon Lake, shimmering blue-green forest jewel. This lake is a rarity in the geologically youthful Coast Range, formed by a landslide -- possibly caused by an earthquake -- that blocked off most of a creek.

This little jaunt you've just concluded -- up Coos River to Allegany, and through the mountains to Loon Lake, not much more than 40 miles -- represented a *full day's* travel in the early decades of the 20th century. Up the rivers on boats and into old Model Ts, rumbling up the rutted roads and walking through the steep parts, helping rebuild plank bridges over wash-outs, and on again to Ash Valley. Reaching Loon Lake was sweet relief, the end of a day's travails. Next day, the families headed down to the Umpqua River, where they ferried over to Scottsburg to continue the trip.

The way skirts along the lake's edge, and if you're here in summer you'll probably spot waterskiers on the water. The road passes a private campground, BLM North Shore campground and a resort. It crosses a bridge over the lake's outlet and encounters BLM Loon Lake campground and day-use area, with a boat ramp, protected swimming area and beach.

At the west end of the beach is a short trail to a little waterfall.

From Loon Lake, the road heads down a canyon of soaring old growth forest, another pocket spared for its diversity and potential wildlife habitat. Continue down the canyon -- a beautiful ride, especially in fall -- to Highway 38 in 7 miles. Turn left (W) to return to Reedsport, 13 miles, and US 101.

11. Riding the Wild Ridges — Lakeside to Dean Creek through Elliott State Forest

Road conditions: *50-mile roundtrip from Lakeside. Mostly gravel.*
Notes: *This is probably the roughest tour in the book, with steep drop-offs and one intense downhill stretch. Watch for logging traffic.*

Here's a tour into the mountains above Lakeside that floats along panoramic ridgelines before plunging down to the Umpqua River not far from Reedsport.

You'll traverse the actively-logged Elliott State Forest, top a watershed divide and drop through a canyon of protected tall timber to emerge at Dean Creek, a pastoral valley that opens onto a protected elk viewing area along Highway 38.

As noted above, this trip's not for the faint of heart, but the really

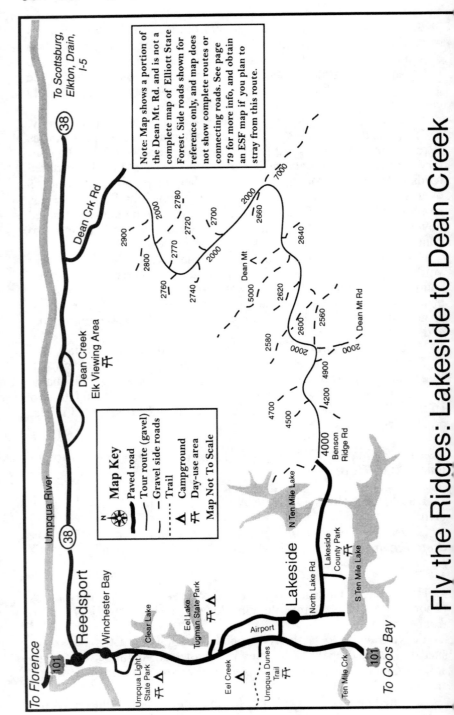

Note: Map shows a portion of the Dean Mt. Rd. and is not a complete map of Elliott State Forest. Side roads shown for reference only, and map does not show complete routes or connecting roads. See page 79 for more info, and obtain an ESF map if you plan to stray from this route.

Fly the Ridges: Lakeside to Dean Creek

steep section only lasts for a couple of miles. This bears repeating: whenever traveling the Elliott State Forest, watch out for log trucks!

Getting There

From the Coos Bay Area, go north on US 101, crossing McCullough Bridge. Continue north for 10 miles, and turn right (E), following signs to Lakeside.

You'll pass a power substation and Lakeside Airport. At a "T" intersection head right (S) over railroad tracks, and into town.

Ten Mile Lakes are among the largest and most developed lakes in dunes country, and the adjacent village of Lakeside is a popular destination for boaters, anglers, campers, and those seeking a quiet place to live. Here are stores, services, marinas, county boat ramps, campgrounds and fishing docks, and plenty of lake to explore. Actually, *two* lakes, connected by a channel, with many homes along the miles of shoreline.

Continue on the main drag (8th St.) into town and turn left (E) on North Lake Rd. Check mileage or zero out your trip odometer here.

The road passes Lakeside's city hall, library and elementary school, along with marinas and lakeshore developments. It crosses a bridge over the channel that connects the lake's two arms, then heads uphill. The road winds past driveways to homes, marinas and resorts, then up through recently logged slopes. There are some fine views, including glimpses of both arms of the lake.

In 4.4 miles, turn right (E) on the gravel 4000 Rd. The road really pushes uphill now, flying above hillsides of clearcuts and plantations, with major views to the north.

There will be many side roads along this route, so maintain a sense for the main road. Stay on the ridgeline road -- watch out for those tremendous drop-offs!

A sign for Elliott State Forest appears at just over the 6-mile mark, and the woods deepen, with ferny cliffs hugging the road. We're just off the ridgeline here, then back on it, with giddy drop-offs to either side.

At 11.8 miles the road forks. Take the left branch, uphill, following 4000 Rd. signs.

At 12.4 miles turn left (N), following signs to the 2000 Rd. We'll be on the 2000 Rd. from here on out.

There are some lofty trees as the road skirts along the ridgeline, riding the roller coaster.

At 14 miles the road forks; stay on the right fork, following the 2000 Rd. Just past that is a grassy overlook, marking the top of the pass, just below Dean Mountain. A side road, gated off, leads to the top of the mountain. You can park here and walk up the road, but there's not much to see since trees atop Dean Mountain block the view.

Here the road begins an immediate descent. A box canyon begins to the east; you can see and hear water rushing down below. A few turns down, at mile 14.9, there's another intersection, with the 7000 Rd.

Turn sharply left (W), following the 2000 Rd.

Big seaward panoramas emerge, and wild rhodies line the gravel route, which is noticeably less used. Isn't this cool? We're really *back there* now, and yet not far off in the west, there's the ocean lying across the horizon. Next is an idyllic stretch where alders form a canopy over the road, green and cool in summer, full of color in fall. Ah, if only that this idyll might last . . . it's as if the roller coaster has clanked and crawled up to its very highest point . . .

And then, here we go! Hang on! The ride downhill includes some serious corkscrew turns and a final white-knuckle ascent of about 3 miles, down and down and down steep canyon faces, through marvelous tall timber. Take it slowly and try to enjoy yourself.

This canyon, another remnant pocket of mature trees in the state forest, has been spared the chainsaw thanks to its status as habitat for endangered spotted owls and marbled murrelets.

At the bottom (22.7 miles), is an Elliott State Forest boundary sign, and just past that, green pastures of Dean Creek Valley.

Pavement begins at 22.8 miles. Turn left (NW) on the county road, weaving along the cutbank river. You can almost feel the clock ticking slower out here. But civilization is getting closer. Pass a big greenhouse operation and in a few moments, at mile 25.5 in this tour, emerge at Highway 38.

Turn left (W) on Highway 38. Just down the road is the Dean Creek Elk Viewing Area, a sanctuary for a wild elk herd, with viewing stations and displays. Can you spot a *dabbling duck?*

A bull elk calls out at the Dean Creek Elk Viewing Area

Continue to Reedsport, 5.5 miles. You'll pass through Reedsport's Old Town, with shops, restaurants, galleries, a waterfront boardwalk and the Umpqua Discovery Center among the attractions. In addition to displays about natural history, the Discovery Center museum has a series of exhibits that follow the theme, "Tidewaters and Time." You can see, hear and touch exhibits that tell the area's history and dependence on waterways.

Continue west to a "T" intersection with US 101 and turn left (S) to return to Lakeside and Coos Bay.

12. Beyond the Loon — Loon Lake/Camp Creek

Road conditions: *Paved, year-round access.*
Notes: *Approximately 75-mile roundtrip from Reedsport. Camping, day-use, fishing, swimming, boating.*

Up in the mountains east of Reedsport is Loon Lake, well known to campers, waterskiers, swimmers, sun-seekers and other summer visitors, but often overlooked as a gateway for forest exploration via a network of paved BLM roads.

The mountain setting of Loon Lake belies its proximity to the coast, and protects it from summer fog and wind. The same summery conditions prevail in the surrounding mountains, with far fewer people!

For this tour, we'll take a scenic, roundabout way to the lake, checking it out toward the end of the loop. Before then, we'll get plenty of solitude, as well as memorable views, plunging waterfalls, and a close encounter with some stately old forest.

Getting There

From Reedsport, go east on Highway 38, following the wide expanse of Umpqua River.

In 3 miles is Dean Creek Elk Viewing Area, home of a resident elk herd and lots of birdlife. Displays offer more information. Next landmark is Umpqua Wayside, a day-use area and boat ramp. A few miles past that is Brandy Bar, so named after the schooner "Samuel Roberts" ran aground in the river here. Seems the crew got into the brandy while waiting for the incoming tide to float the boat free.

You might spot river dredges working in this vicinity, drawing up loads of gravel.

About 13 miles from Reedsport, turn right (S), on Mill Creek Rd., following signs to Loon Lake Recreation Area.

The road heads up Mill Creek, a trickle in summer and fall, rushing torrent in winter. The canyon has been spared from logging, and there's a wonderful mix of trees. Stately maples along the creek sport thick coats of moss, and in autumn they blaze with color. The wildflower

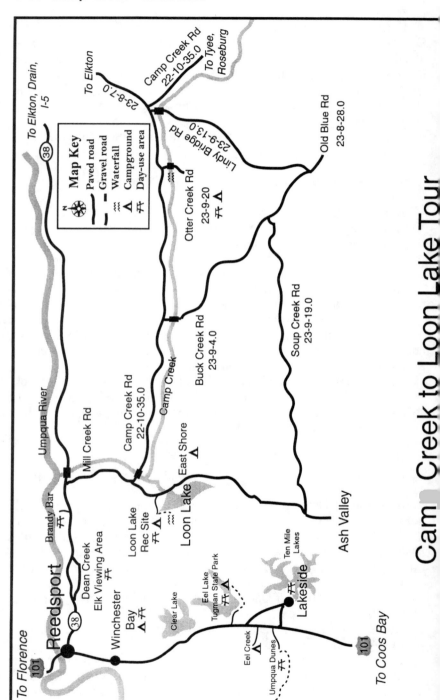

Camp Creek to Loon Lake Tour

show can be tremendous. In addition to foxglove, Indian paintbrush, tiger lilies and daises, you might spot the pink heads of valerians, or bleeding hearts, yellow monkey flowers, red columbine and creamy fawn lilies, among others.

On display in rocky cliffs and crannies are hanging gardens of tiny succulent stonecrops, blooming well into the summer. They survive the hot, dry months by storing water in their leaves, and belong to the genus *sedum*, sometimes called "liveforever."

The lake is 7 miles up, but we'll be turning off before then.

Just over 5 miles up, turn left (E) on Camp Creek Rd., BLM 22-10-35.0. Note your mileage or zero out your trip odometer here.

Cross the river and follow placid Camp Creek through a canopy of alder trees. Tiny waterfalls spill down from the hills, and mossy cliffs hug the road. The river runs through corridors of trees -- alder, maple, myrtle, fir, cedar, hemlock -- and there are little pools and rapids. You might spot weirs of rocks or timbers slanting across the river; these slow down stream flows and allow gravel beds to recover for spawning fish.

There's a gravel quarry along the road, and evidence of logging on the upper hillsides. Scotch broom, an invasive non-native plant spreading its reach, flourishes in disturbed areas. You'll pass Buck Creek Rd., BLM 23-9-4.0, about 6.8 miles along. Just over 11 miles is a paved road to the right that leads to Camp Creek Falls. It's not marked along the road, but there's a sign in few hundred feet, BLM 23-9-20. About 0.2 mile along, turn right to a parking area. There are a few primitive campsites adjacent to the waterfalls, a pretty, multi-tiered cascade with a pool at the bottom for swimming and splashing.

Back on Camp Creek Rd., at 14 miles is a "T" intersection, with signs indicating the way left to Elkton on Little Camp Creek Rd., BLM 23-8-7.0., and right to Roseburg on what becomes BLM 22-10-35.0.

Just before this intersection, turn right (S) on a paved road that crosses a concrete bridge and heads uphill. If intact, signs identify this as Lindy Bridge Rd., BLM 23-9-13.0.

Once across the bridge, the road heads up through big trees and climbs toward an expanding panorama. At 16.6 miles is a Lindy Bridge Rd. sign. At 17.8 miles is an intersection with signs directing you to Loon Lake, 10 miles, as well as Old Blue Rd. and Camp Creek Rd. Turn right (N) on Buck Creek Rd., BLM 23-9-4.0. More spectacular views and nice trees! At 18.5 miles turn left (W) on Soup Creek Rd., BLM 23-9-19.0, following a sign to Loon Lake, 9 miles.

Pause at this intersection and gaze to the northwest corner. That is one awesome old fir, one of the largest in the vicinity. There are a number of other old-growth specimens here, too.

The route roller-coasts down through grand forestlands. The area around Remmy Creek, about 2 miles down, is closed to vehicles to pro-

Three-tiered waterfall and inviting pool along Camp Creek

tect a rich mix of flora and fauna and those nice big trees. The stillness of the remote woods is broken occasionally by joyous birdsong.

At about 21 miles into the tour, you'll come to the fringes of Ash Valley and signs of civilization. Pass a couple of roads on the left -- Slideout Creek Rd. and Soup Creek Ridge Rd. Stick to pavement.

Cross a cattle guard and watch out for cows along the roadway. Cross another guard and at mile 22 you'll encounter a road to the right signed as North Fork Soup Creek Rd., BLM 23-9-19.1.

Take the left fork, which now sports a double-yellow line and is identified as Douglas County Rd. 72. Follow it to mile 23.2 and a "T" intersection with Mill Creek County Rd., Douglas County Rd. 3. You'll turn right (N) here, but first take a little detour in the other direction, just up the road to the former site of Ash, a village named after the trees here. All that's left is the whitewashed and red-trimmed Ash Valley School, but there was once a community complete with such things as a cheese factory and sawmill.

Turn around and head north on Mill Creek Rd., and before long you'll be skirting the edge of Loon Lake. There are limited services here, including a private campground, resort and two BLM campgrounds. Adjacent to the BLM campground at the north end of the lake is a sandy beach for sunning and swimming, as well as boat ramp. The lake is also popular with waterskiers and personal watercraft enthusiasts.

Loon Lake was named in 1852 by explorers who saw a floating log with a loon's nest containing two eggs. Two loons were hovering nearby, but the men scooped up the eggs, packed them in moss and eventually turned them over to a scientific academy for study.

Loons still frequent the lake, sending out their distinctive, plaintive cry around dusk.

The lake's outlet at the north end spills into Mill Creek, which the road crosses on a bridge just before the BLM site.

From there, it's all downhill through a canyon of lofty old forest. A few miles down you'll pass Camp Creek Rd. on the right (E), where part of this tour began. Stay on Mill Creek Rd., heading downhill to return to Highway 38, and turn left (W) to return to Reedsport and US 101.

13. The Old Way — Coos Bay Wagon Road

Road conditions: *Two unpaved sections. Muddy after snow or rain, dusty in summer. Occasionally closed in winter by snow at higher elevations.*

Notes: *120-mile roundtrip from Coos Bay. Best in late spring, during wildflower bloom, or after first autumn rains, for leafy colors. Wagon Road changes names a few times along the way, but destinations are clearly indicated. Camping, day-use, fishing.*

This is a pioneer land route from Coos Bay to Roseburg, still unpaved in two places, but a real treasure of the region. You'll pass waterfalls roiling right along the road, weave through old-growth forest, traverse idyllic valleys and pass historic farmsteads, and emerge in the rolling pasturelands and wine country of the Umpqua Valley.

The trip's not that much farther in miles than the main road -- Hghway

Waterfall roils and roars alongside Coos Bay Wagon Road

42 -- to Roseburg, but definitely slower going. It twists through many undulations of the Coast Range, climbing in and out of small valleys over a series of ridges. A few remnants of the old wagon days remain, and there are little communities along the way, as well as campgrounds, parks, and picnic areas both official and impromptu.

You can get to the Wagon Road from a number of places on its route from Coos Bay to Lookkingglass, near Roseburg. The Wagon Road bears that name at both ends, but it changes names a few times along the way to reflect the towns through which it passes. It's pretty well signed, especially at intersections that lead to connecting arteries.

The initial stretch from Coos Bay passes through rural residential areas and takes on a mean bit of gravel road, so you might consider starting the trek from Fairview, via Coquille. Refer to chapter 16 for directions to Coquille and Fairview. What follows are directions from the official Coos Bay terminus of the Wagon Road.

Getting There
From the south end of Coos Bay on US 101, go left at the "Y" following the sign to Allegany, Coos River. The road crosses a bridge over railroad tracks and another over Isthmus Slough. Once across Isthmus Slough Bridge turn right (S) on Olive Barber Rd. The road passes one of the few operating sawmills in Coos Bay as it weaves along the hills above Isthmus Slough. About 2 miles from the bridge, turn left (E) on Wagon Road.

It begins a familiar pattern, corkscrewing up into the hills. The road

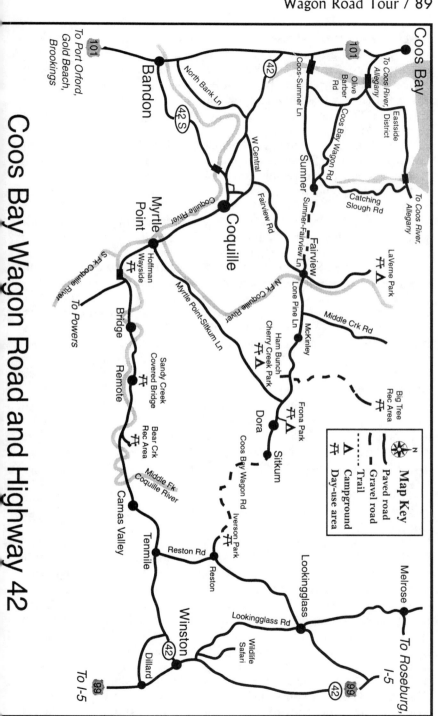

Coos Bay Wagon Road and Highway 42

passes many homes and residential side streets, then drops down to Ross Inlet. Keep going east on Wagon Road as it heads over another ridge, ascending into wetlands and pastures of Catching Slough. The road encounters Catching Slough Rd. 6.8 miles from the start of Wagon Road, and together they head to an intersection with Coos-Sumner Ln.

Turn left (E) on Coos-Sumner Ln., following the sign to Sumner, Fairview. And here's Sumner.

The Wagon Road originally began (or ended, depending on your direction of travel) in Sumner, which is near the head of Catching Slough. Passengers and freight would travel on riverboats from towns around the bay up the slough to Sumner, where the 58-mile journey began. Fare was $6.25.

The trip could take as long as *three days,* depending on snow conditions at higher elevations. On the best of days, with no delays, the wagon trip took 28 hours. Wayside houses along the route served travelers and kept fresh horses. Settlements grew in the valleys, and carry on a bucolic existence to this day, evidenced by homesteads historic and motley.

There's a general store in Sumner, along with a cluster of houses and farms spread out over the valley and hills. The road (now called Sumner-Fairview Ln.) arrows through the valley and up a canyon, turning to gravel in 1 mile. There are some mean switchbacks! Just take it slowly and enjoy this section, little changed for over 130 years. You'll pass small waterfalls and gigantic swordferns, and the first of many fine old trees you'll be enjoying on this trip.

The road levels out through a remote stretch of clearcut and regrowth forest, with many lesser roads coming in. Keep to the well-traveled but still gravel Wagon Road. Pavement returns at the crest of the ridge and the road descends to Fairview. You'll pass farms and houses, and 1927-era Fairview School, and come to the Four Corners intersection. A grocery store has supplies.

To the right (S) is Coquille (9 miles); to the left (N) is LaVerne County Park (7 miles), with camping and a day-use area with a sandy beach and swimming hole.

Go straight (E), on what's now called Lone Pine Ln., following signs to Middle Creek Rd., Dora and McKinley. This valley was named Burton Prairie for pioneer Eliza Burton, and came to be known as Fairview because from the hillside waystation, you could get a "fair view."

There's a power substation in Fairview, and you may have already noticed the highlines marching along the valleys and ridges. The towers follow much of the Wagon Road route. The Wagon Road is also the proposed route of a natural gas pipeline, the installation of which may change certain aspects of this trip or cause travel delays.

Still paved, the road crosses a concrete bridge and heads up into the hills again. There are some big trees, as well as clearcut areas that open up grand vistas. The road drops down into a valley, passing Middle Creek

Vintage slide in Dora County Park recalls simpler times

Rd. (See chapter 17.)

In another mile is a feeder road from Myrtle Point and Norway. Next is McKinley — a few scattered homes — and site of William Ham Bunch/Cherry Creek County Park, a grove of aromatic myrtlewoods that sigh in counterpoint to the rush of the adjacent stream. There are primitive camping sites, for a fee.

Directly across the road from Cherry Creek Park is the road to BLM

Big Tree recreation site. This is a potential out-and-back detour (less than 10 miles roundtrip) from Wagon Road. The first 2 miles of road are gravel. The route is well marked.

The Big Tree (also called Forest Giant) was once thought to be the largest coastal Douglas fir, but was felled by a root disease in the 1990s. It's imposing even on its side, lying amidst a wondrous canyon of mixed-species, old-growth forest in a magical USFS day-use area. (See chapter 17 for other details.)

Continuing on the Wagon Road from Cherry Creek Park, the road passes McKinley Grange, then – *here we go!* The route heads uphill through five very snarly turns. Imagine going up or coming down this road in a wagon! Side roads enter from both directions as the road tops off, but stick to pavement. The road drops down through a clearcut to a "Y" intersection and stop sign. To the right is a road to Myrtle Point. Continue east, to Dora and Sitkum.

Next landmark is Frona County Park, offering picnicking and primitive camping. Check out the vintage playground equipment saved from the old Dora School and note especially the lettering on the footsteps of that big old slide!

Not far past the park is a classic old house. It was built as a stage stop, but the coaches stopped running before the house was completed in 1922.

You'll then encounter Dora, with the library, school and fire station all in one building down the lone sidestreet. There's also a general store in Dora, last for many miles.

The road traverses the valley floor, with the river bubbling through thick alder groves. The canopy is cool and green in summer, a showy spectacle in autumn, stark in winter.

Now we're going to start climbing, with the road narrowing to a single lane in places. The river churns dramatically right alongside, muddy brown in winter and pea-soup green in summer. Sheer rocks rise along the other side of the road, and the hulking big-leaf maples are thick with moss from constant spray.

Yet another ridgeline crested, and here is Brewster Valley, named for an early white settler. With its shimmering natural meadows and surrounding mountain domes of richly mixed timber, it was heralded in frontier times as one of the most beautiful, pristine valleys in the region. Some pioneers simply stopped their westward quest, figuring it wouldn't get any better.

Historian O.O. Dodge said its "wild state resembled a beautiful picnic ground, the elegant tall myrtles and maples forming shady dells where twilight seemed to linger at midday."

The settlement here is Sitkum, Chinook Indian word for *half*. Established in 1872, there was a stage stop that served as hotel, tavern, restaurant and livery stable. Travelers spent the night, as under normal circumstances it was a full day's ride to either Roseburg or Coos Bay.

Nothing's left of the old stage stop, but you can glimpse Sitkum School to the right, with gym (now a barn) and one-time teacher's residence.

The road turns to gravel here, both the roughest and most awe-inspiring part of the trip. Remember to take it slowly, use the turnouts if necessary, and be alert!

There are literally waterfalls on top of waterfalls through here, a series of them right along the road. Mammoth trees hug the byway and jut at dizzying angles from escarpments high overhead. There are pullouts where you can stop to check out each waterfall.

The road continues up through the alders, gradually leveling out. Pavement begins about 10 miles past Sitkum, at the Douglas County line.

The road, now with double yellow stripes and fog lines, heads through regrowth forest and then down through grand woodlands, with brief views of the valley to the east.

Iverson County Park comes along after a couple of miles. Then you'll swoop down through a cutover area, around hairpin turns, suddenly emerging amidst rolling pastures.

4 miles from the summit at a "T" intersection is Reston, site of the only remaining waystation, the Arthur Johnson Farm and Stage House, built in 1911. That's it with the red metal roof. The barn was built so the stage could be driven in one side, the horses changed, then exit through the other door. It's a private residence, but there are interpretive signs.

In case you're wondering, the name Reston does indeed have to do with *rest,* since that's what early travelers did here. Seems there already was a Rest, Ore., so they called it Reston.

A turn right (S) on Reston Rd. will take you in 5 miles to Tenmile, on Highway 42, on which you can return to Coos County. There's also a blue sign here pointing the way to Giradet Winery, part of the winery tour, about which more in a moment.

Keep going straight to continue to Lookingglass, Roseburg, Interstate 5, or to nearby attractions such as the Wildlife Game Park in Winston or the other wineries.

There are six wineries in the Roseburg vicinity, all well marked by blue winery tour signs. Some are open year-'round, others seasonally or by appointment. Wine tour brochure with maps are available at visitor centers, wineries and in informational-literature racks in Douglas County.

Continuing east on Wagon Road, you'll pass numerous farms and ranches, and a unique octagonal barn. Built in the 1870s by James Wilmer, the eight-sided shape creates more usable floor space with the same amount of material as a rectangular structure.

The Wagon Road terminates in Lookingglass, so named for the mirror-like shimmering of surrounding grasslands. The road comes to a "T" intersection here, across from an Old West-style general store.

To get to Roseburg and I-5, turn left (N) and follow signs.

To complete this loop, turn right (S) on Lookingglass Rd. and proceed to Highway 42. Turn right and head into Winston. You'll see the access road to Wildlife Safari Game Park. This 600-acre preserve features a walk-around wildlife village, gift shop and restaurant, as well as an acclaimed drive-through area with tigers, cheetah, hippos, rhinos, elephants, giraffes, primates and many types of birds. It's open all year.

At the stoplight in Winston, turn right (W) on Highway 42 to the Oregon Coast. Highway 42, originally called the Coos Bay Military Road, replaced the Wagon Road as the main thoroughfare in the 1920s. It's a flyer, busy with chip and log trucks, RVs, rigs pulling boats and locals hurrying between inland and coastal communities.

Once clear of Winston, Highway 42 makes a straight shot past rural homes and ranches, passing the local high school before rolling the countryside. About 10 miles out is appropriately-named Tenmile. Here, too, is Reston Rd. to the right (N) and Giradet Winery, with vineyards and tasting room.

Just beyond Tenmile is an access road to Ben Irving Reservoir, where day-use activities include swimming, fishing and boating.

Highway 42 begins the climb up 1472-ft Camas Mountain, once an arduous part of the route made better in recent years by highway improvements. The road tops the ridge and descends into Camas Valley, named as are many communities in the Pacific Northwest for a plant in the lily family that grows in marshy areas. Its bulbs were a food source for Indians, trappers and settlers.

The road cuts across Camas Valley, about the halfway point in the Roseburg-Coos Bay trek on Highway 42. But many more curves remain to be negotiated as the road more or less follows the westward meanders of the Coquille River's middle fork. The road crosses and recrosses the river, climbing ridges and shoulders of the Coast Range.

BLM Bear Creek recreation site offers day-use, with access to the river and a seasonally active waterfall.

Despite the well-traveled highway, this is lonely country. And despite highway improvements, there are some tight turns. Just when you seem to be miles into the middle of nowhere – and you *are* – here's civilization again, a tiny settlement appropriately enough called Remote. The general store has some historical displays, and on the north side of Highway 42 is a day-use area with a restored covered wooden bridge. Check this out: there are picnic tables *right on the bridge!*

Then it's back into the woods again, with Highway 42 more definitively following the river now. Next settlement is Bridge, with a general store and café. The highway follows the river the remaining 9 miles to Myrtle Point, and from there onto Coquille and US 101.

(For details about Myrtle Point and Coquille, see chapter 14.)

14. Local Farm Time — Coquille Valley

Road conditions: *Paved, except for two short gravel sections. Subject to winter flooding.*
Notes: *About 100 miles roundtrip from Coos Bay. Seasonal camping, day-use, fishing, boating, swimming.*

The town of Coquille spreads across high ground above the Coquille Valley, about 20 miles inland from the coast. Its heydays -- as turn-of-the-century river boomtown and later as thriving logging center -- have faded, but the fact that it's still the county seat, and still surrounded by productive farmlands and ranches, keeps the town humming along.

The river here is also called Coquille, and it regularly overtops its banks in winter and spring, inundating lowland pastures and back roads. Sometimes the damage is worse, such as in 1996, when record rainfall flooded homes and farms.

Locals call the vast stretch of flooded fields Winter Lake, but if you're here in summer or fall, all you'll see are green pastures dotted with grazing cattle and horses.

At the other end of the Coquille River Valley is Myrtle Point, also with a history dating to pioneer days and about which more later. The two towns, and the farmland between, are in some ways time capsules from another era. Most folks can trace some connection with early settlers, including Indians.

And while the towns may bustle with activity and traffic hurries by on Highway 42, within sight of both life slows comfortably to what I call Local Farm Time. It's another world entirely; another way, an old way. Things seem more understandable out here. Cow eats grass, cow gives milk. Horse rubs old fence post. Sleepy dog continues nap. Rooster crows at nothing in particular.

And there's an old road, appropriately enough. Unhurried, going the back way to Myrtle Point and thence to Broadbent, with a detour up a little country lane just for fun.

A ride through the countryside can be downright relaxing. Therapeutic, I tellya.

Getting There
From Coos Bay, head south on US 101. At the "Y" about 5 miles south, take the left fork, (Highway 42) following signs to Coquille. The road continues along Isthmus Slough, passing the settlement of Greenacres before crossing a low rise and dropping into Coquille Valley.

You'll pass Coaledo, named for early-day mining activities.

Coquille comes along about 16 miles from Coos Bay. For this tour, we'll be taking a turn off the Highway 42 bypass of Coquille, but if you want a look at the town, take the West Coquille turnoff (West Central

Blvd.) off Highway 42 as you enter town and refer to the following section.

Coquille: The West Coquille turnoff follows the old route of Highway 42. The road rolls past homes, mobile home parks and businesses, and the high school. The road tops a hill at a stoplight before dropping into the main part of town.

Coquille is the Coos County seat, with the county courthouse, jail and other county offices making up part of the downtown area. There are some well-preserved homes in the neighborhoods around the courthouse and above the Safeway store.

The better-known homes include the Maune House, built in 1888, at First and Dean Streets; the Judge Harlocker House, built in 1891 and surrounded by myrtlewood trees, and the Bonney House, 1901, both at South Collier and Main. The Coquille Chamber of Commerce office at the foot of 2nd St. (next to the library and senior center) has a map to historic homes.

Downtown are a few classic old buildings, built of brick and dating back to the late 1800s and early 1900s. Among them is the Coquille Valley *Sentinel* building (1905), which has memorabilia and old papers on display. Adding to a vintage touch are creatively painted storefronts and murals of old-time street scenes.

The boom a century ago was fueled by speculation that the railroad link from Coos Bay would continue east to Roseburg. The railroad eventually chose a northerly route, but Coquille Valley continued to prosper, thanks to the fertile farmlands and seemingly limitless forests.

The downturn in the timber economy took Coquille along with it, although one sawmill continues to operate at this writing, and there are other small industries. In addition to its county seat status, Coquille is a bedroom community for the Coos Bay Area. Locals like to say housing is more affordable "and it's not so windy!"

Hard to believe that less than 150 years ago, most of this was "tangled forest and vine maple, brake and bramble vine," according to one local historian. "Its outlet to the world was alone by the ever-ready canoe."

First white settler was Evan Cunningham, who later started a quill-written newspaper, The Coquille *Microcosm*, and served as first county schools superintendent.

How the name came to be remains a topic of spirited debate, taking up three-quarters of a page in McArthur's *Oregon Geographic Names*. A French sea captain supposedly saw native shell mounds, and called the place *Coquelle*, an early French spelling for *coquille*, or "shell."

Historians and residents -- including Native Americans -- disagree. One pioneer insisted it should be *Scoquille*, the name given to large schools of eels (actually lampreys). Historian Nathan Douthit notes several words in local Indian languages sounded similar to the present name, and they may have referred to the river or the Indians, called by some

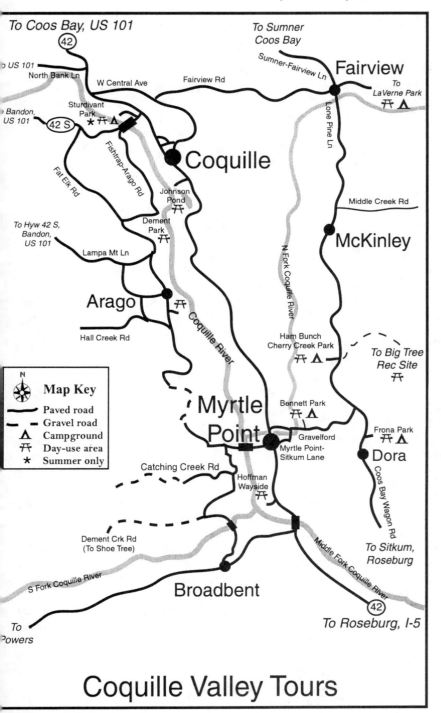

Coquille Valley Tours

"Ku-Kwil-tunne." Other Indian names ranged from *Scoquel* to *Kiguel* to *Coquilth*, with differences in pronunciation that exist to this day. For instance, locals call the town "Koe-keel," while the local Indian tribe are "Koe-qwell," though both spell it Coquille.

After you've had a look at Coquille, return to Highway 42. From the downtown district, turn right (W) on 42 and in about 0.5 mile turn left (S) on Highway 42S. Directions continue in the following section.

If you have chosen to skip the Coquille tour, proceed on Highway 42 and turn right (S) on Highway 42S, following signs to Bandon.

Just this side of the river is Sturdivant Park, with seasonal camping, picnic area and boat launch. There's some early-day logging and mill equipment on display, and a plaque commemorating the contribution of 28,883 "Spruce Soldiers" who worked in the woods and logging camps getting trees that were used to make airplanes in WWI.

Follow Highway 42S and cross the bridge over the Coquille River. Immediately across the bridge exit 42S onto Arago-Fishtrap Rd., which loops underneath the bridge approach.

In pioneer days, the river was the main thoroughfare. A busy commercial district with wharves and landings sat on pilings along the water's edge. A fleet of riverboats plied the Coquille, and small, ocean-going schooners brought goods from San Francisco and other ports, and left with loads of logs, lumber and farm goods. Today, only old foundations and rotted pilings remain, best viewed from this side of the river.

The road roams through the countryside, past homesteads that range from the unkempt to the neatly kept. Folks out here relish their collections of vintage farm equipment, and fortunately the pace is relaxed enough so you can slow down and get a good look at the rusting relics.

In 2.5 miles is Wallace Dement Myrtlewood Grove, a thick myrtle stand along a mile-long riverfront preserve. It's a day-use county park offering fishing access and picnicking. This grove was typical of valley land a century ago, when farmers struggled to clear the robust hardwood today so prized for carving. Noted early-day historian A.G. Walling: "It grows in such vast quantities no demand could ever arise that could not be fully met." If myrtle trees are cut but the stumps not removed, they'll grow back; some of the massive specimens in this grove represent "second growth" of previously cut myrtles!

Beyond Dement Grove 0.5 mile is a "T" intersection. Turn left (SE), following signs to Arago, Fishtrap Creek and Myrtle Point. Settlers coined the term Fishtrap for Indian fish weirs along here. While the Indians were pretty clever about catching fish in the basket-like weirs, early white settlers *really* went at it. Local author Lee Stonecypher, in his book "These Fast Changing Times," recalls fishermen using drift nets to bring in as much as *20 tons* per day of silver salmon, or "shiners." He wrote: "They were there by the millions and you could put hooks on a line and catch two or three at a time, which was not against the law."

The road skirts above the river plain, giving a good look at cutbanks that attest to the river's winter fury. The river giveth and taketh, however; as one history book notes, "although the high freshets overflow the land . . . the soil is sufficiently renovated thereby to compensate for all damage done."

At the next "Y" intersection, veer left, staying on Arago-Fishtrap Rd. The road dips down to the settlement of Arago, named as is Cape Arago in honor of French physician and geographer Dominique Francois Jean Arago.

Next is Arago boat ramp, with picnic tables and restrooms.

Past that a bit is a "T" intersection with Lampa Ln. Go left, following signs to Myrtle Point. The road again skirts the valley floor, eventually arriving at a spot across the river from Myrtle Point. We'll get there in roundabout fashion.

Cross the concrete bridge towards Myrtle Point, then turn right (SE) on Old Broadbent Rd., immediately crossing another bridge.

Note your odometer reading here. The road drifts again into soothing countryside, the river hugging close by. In 1.5 miles turn right (S) on Catching Creek Ln. The sign may be missing, so be alert for this paved county road. There's an old wooden platform above the river just across from Catching Creek Ln.

The road meanders up into the hills and dead-ends at private ranch roads in about 10 miles, but it's a fun detour that we'll end at an old country chapel and graveyard.

Head up the road through sleepy pastures and trees full of Spanish moss. The hillsides are thick with alders that glow with greenery in spring and summer, and blaze with fall color. The road turns to gravel 5 miles up.

Fires in the mid-1800s devastated this region. In the denuded landscape early settlers saw "prairies" for free-ranging livestock. The tradition continues to this day, except that the cattle, horses, sheep, goats, llamas, ostriches, emus, geese, ducks and turkeys are (usually) confined by fences.

About 2 miles more is a yurt house up on the hill to the left, and just ahead on the right is the old whitewashed Marsters Chapel, once a schoolhouse and United Brethren church. Behind the chapel is Catching Creek Cemetery, with headstones dating to 1884.

The gravel road ends a few miles up at private property, so turn around here at the chapel and head back.

At the intersection with Old Broadbent Rd., turn right. The road encounters two short gravel sections on its way to Broadbent.

At the next "T" intersection, with Dement Creek Rd., turn left (N), toward Broadbent. (Note: If you wish to see the "shoe tree" pictured in

Whimsical "shoe tree" in Coquille Valley countryside

this chapter, turn right (S) on Dement Creek Rd. The road turns to gravel. The shoe tree is on the left side in 1.6 miles. Use caution, as this road leads to a gravel quarry and is heavily used by trucks and local traffic.)

Meantime, back on Old Broadbent Rd: it zags through ranchlands, crosses a concrete bridge and comes to a "T" intersection at Walter Donald Rd. Turn right (E). You'll pass the whitewashed Broadbent school-house, and come to Powers Highway.

Broadbent's sleepiness belies a colorful history. Named for cheese maker C.E. Broadbent, its earliest residents were a group of from Baltimore, Md., whose leader, Dr. Henry Hermann, had searched the west for land to colonize with family and friends.

On "discovering" the upper Coquille Valley, Hermann returned to Maryland and brought back kith and kin, many of whom were German immigrants and whose numbers included a mechanic, cabinet maker, tinner and blacksmith, in addition to the good doctor. They shared a keen interest in farming. "All the elements to start a community," proclaimed an early history.

Arriving in 1859, members of the Baltimore Colony built homes, planted crops and established livestock and bees. They had success growing everything from artichokes to flaxseed, and their first export crop -- also sometimes said to be Coos County's first export crop -- was tobacco. Grown from Cuban seed, typical yield was 1,500 to 2,000 pounds per acre, and "Coquille Leaf" was shipped by the ton to San Francisco.

Elton Schroeder, grandson of a founding member of the Baltimore Colony, said in interview for this book that some of the settlers had lived on farms in Maryland where tobacco was raised from the earliest generations of the American colonies. They applied their skills with this crop to their newly colonized land on the West Coast.

Many Baltimore colonists played musical instruments, and they formed a band complete with fancy uniforms. One music lover brought in the region's first piano, having it shipped 'round the Horn. Like many goods of the era, after arriving by ship in Coos Bay the piano was rafted up Isthmus Slough, then packed by Indian women over the watershed divide to the Coquille River. The piano was loaded back onto a boat -- from which it fell overboard and was retrieved -- and taken upriver to Broadbent, where it entertained people for years. Current whereabouts unknown, alas.

Leaving the Broadbent road, turn left (N) on Powers Highway, heading back to Highway 42 in 2.5 miles. Once at Highway 42, turn left (NW) to return to the Coos Bay Area.

Myrtle Point, also rich with pioneer history, is just around the corner. Classic old buildings date back to the feverish days of 1890s. Six remaining buildings on Spruce Street date from that era. You can also see some of the early-day splendor in a few of the residences around the downtown district.

Here, as in Coquille, the railroad's decision on an alternate route didn't doom the town. Rich agricultural lands and forests still maintain the economy; an oft-repeated local claim suggests there's never been a crop failure in Coos County.

A favorite place is the old American Legion Hall, now the Coos County Logging Museum, just one block off Highway 42, at 7th and Maple Street. Built in the 'Teens as a scaled-down replica of the Mormon Tabernacle in Salt Lake City, the domed building failed to achieve the Tabernacle's fabled acoustics and in fact has a variety of weird effects on sounds and speech. Depending on where you're speaking -- or listening -- the sound eerily bounces or deadens, and although this aggravated early-day parishioners, as well as others such as Legionnaires who subsequently tried to use the building, it's great fun, especially considering this is a museum.

On that subject, there's a fascinating collection of early-day logging equipment, and you can touch and hold some of the old tools of the trade. The vintage photos are absorbing. The museum keeps regular hours in summer.

Across the street from the museum, to the west, is a huge, double-trunked myrtlewood tree, one of the largest of its kind. It's part of a walking tour of trees in Myrtle Point, a guide to which you can pick up at the museum or city hall.

If you're in town on a Sunday, you might also stop in at St. Ann and Michael's Catholic Church, Second and Ash Streets. The interior is finished exclusively in myrtlewood, all taken from a single tree.

In the days before whites arrived, this area on high banks near the three forks of the Coquille River was a gathering place for natives, a "place they lived while away from the seashore, a place to chase . . . the elk that roamed the hillsides and the spacious, shady dells," as M.G. Pohl explained in a 1903 newspaper article.

When you're through exploring Myrtle Point, continue west on Highway 42, to Coquille and the Coos Bay Area.

Your return will take you past the tiny settlement of Norway, which is actually the second location of this town. The original site across the river, founded by Norwegian immigrants, had a large store with a hall on the second floor for dances and social events. For a few years, Norway was the liveliest town on the upper river.

Returning on Highway 42, a few miles beyond Norway is the Johnson Mill Pond, now a park administered by the Port of Bandon. This 112-acre lake, built to store logs for a downriver mill, is open for day-use. There's a small pier for fishing, and although there's no boat ramp, you can launch a car-topper, canoe or kayak here, and swimming is allowed. Trails and dirt roads follow the west and south sides of the pond. A trail is being planned that would go along the old railroad right-of-way into Coquille.

Not far beyond, on Highway 42 heading toward Coquille, is the Coquille Valley Art Center, with displays and activities.

The road continues to Coquille, and from there returns to US 101 and the Coos Bay Area.

15.   The Other Back Way – Coquille Tour Two

Road conditions: *Paved except for 2-mile gravel stretch of road on suggested side-trip.*
Notes: *About 100 miles roundtrip from Coos Bay. Camping, day-use, fishing, swimming.*

Here's another back-road tour in the countryside between Coquille and Myrtle Point. It's great in spring when everything is greening-up, and summertime brings an even more relaxing pace. In autumn, the changing colors of big leafy maples and other deciduous trees add a delicious touch. There are a couple of county parks along the way where you can stop for a picnic, as well as a potential side-trip to another day-use picnic area where you'll find one of the world's largest trees.

Getting There

From Coos Bay, head south on US 101 about 5 miles and take Highway 42 to Coquille. Take the first Coquille exit (West Central Blvd.), following signs to LaVerne Park. In 1 mile turn left on Fairview Rd., following signs to Fairview, LaVerne Park.

Relax! The road rambles into the country, passing pastures and fields where cows, horses, sheep and goats sometimes all browse in peaceful proximity of each other. You'll go by some showplace farms and ranches (and a few of the other kind) before climbing out of the valley. Continue about 7.5 miles to the Fairview junction. The store here is your last chance for supplies for a while.

A highlight of Fairview is the old whitewashed schoolhouse, just west of the junction.

Turn right (E) at the Fairview junction on Lone Pine Lane. This is part of the Coos Bay Wagon Road, original land route into the region, twisting through the undulations of the Coast Range, and negotiating a series of small valleys such as the one here in Fairview.

The road goes by an electric power substation, crosses a bridge and heads uphill, snaking through the forest in classic Wagon Road fashion. If you're here in autumn, you'll notice the vine maple in hues of gold and red hugging the road, and maple trees adding a golden mantle to the woodland greenery.

A swath cut for powerlines opens a brief view north, while a clearcut farther up offers wide western panoramas.

The Wagon Road crests, and as you descend you'll enjoy big views east. The forest is a checkerboard of trees, clearcuts and recently-re-planted ("reprod") areas. A few mountaintops stick up here and there in the sea of trees.

Plunge down through reprod forest into a narrow east-west canyon that holds a handful of tall trees. Pass Middle Creek Rd. (for a tour out this way, see chapter 17.)

The valley widens to reveal the community of McKinley, with country places scattered here and there. A bit beyond (7 miles from Fairview) is William A. Ham Bunch/Cherry Creek County Park. Named both for an early-day school superintendent *and* the nearby creek, the park has picnicking, primitive camping and restrooms in a grove of huge, aromatic myrtlewood trees. The swiftly-running yet quietly soothing waters of Cherry Creek are close at hand.

For a detour to BLM Big Tree recreation site, turn left (N) on Cherry Creek Rd., directly across from the county park. The road is gravel for about 2 miles, but not too bad. It's fairly level and straight as it heads up a small river canyon, passing farmsteads and homes. The road is dotted here and there -- and wonderfully lined in other places -- with maple trees that produce a cool canopy of leaves in spring and summer, and a golden autumn show in September and October.

Just under 2 miles up pavement returns, and a sign identifies this as Cherry Creek Rd., BLM 27-11-27.0. Also on the sign is an arrow pointing the way ahead to Big Tree. The road -- considerably narrower now -- continues to follow the canyon, with Cherry Creek flowing on the right. At about 3 miles, bear left at a "Y" intersection, following a sign to Big Tree. The road's about as wide as a driveway, lined with cedars to the left and alders to the right, a bucolic forest lane.

At 4.2 miles the road crosses a little bridge. The creek's on the left now as the road continues its gradual climb. The climb becomes more pronounced, and suddenly, here's Big Tree recreation site.

What a storybook place! A path leads down from the parking area to a few picnic tables and an interpretive sign about the Big Tree. The sign explains that the tree, once known as the Forest Giant and believed to be the largest coastal Douglas fir in the world, was cut down in 1996 after it was diagnosed with a root disease. The tree was felled and left in place, and may still be one of the largest firs -- just no longer living.

You can follow the trail across the bridge and up the hill to the Big Tree, or take a short loop trail that gives you a good look at the incredibly diverse woodlands. This diversity, in fact, has led the BLM to designate this an "area of critical environmental concern," sparing it for the moment from logging and setting it aside for study and limited recreation.

From the Big Tree recreation site, retrace your route back down Cherry Creek Rd. to the Wagon Road. Turn left (E) on Wagon Road, following signs to Dora. You'll pass McKinley Grange, then — *hold on!* The road twists uphill around five *very* tight turns. Imagine the wagons going up (or coming down!) these turns in the old days . . .

The road crests out and heads downhill on a rather tame straight-away. In moments (just 1.7 miles from Cherry Creek, in fact), the Wagon Road comes to an intersection. Turn right (S), following the sign to Myrtle Point, 17 miles.

More fine, fine countryside and smooth autumn color. About 1 mile along you'll pass Dora Cemetery, dating to 1886 and featuring some grave markers made from Port Orford cedar. Apropos to the region, the forest was recently clearcut right to the fenceline of the cemetery, and the next generation of trees has been planted.

The road -- following the Coquille River's north fork now -- settles into a relaxing ramble. If you're here in summer, the fields and pastures are awash in many shades of green; in autumn the foliage and trees are lit up in luminous golden tones.

About 11 miles along is Gravelford. Just before the bridge, you can turn right on the gravel road marked by a sign that identifies it as the route to Bennett Park and Lee Valley. Bennett County Park is about 0.4 mile down this road, and is another quiet little park set in a grove of trees along the river. So many parks to picnic in . . .

At any rate, continue from Gravelford toward Myrtle Point. You'll cross the North Fork again; keep following signs to Myrtle Point. The road rolls through more enchanting country, but pretty soon the houses start getting closer together, and all of a sudden, here you are in Myrtle Point, at Highway 42. (For more information about Myrtle Point, see chapter 14.)

Turn right to return on Highway 42 to Coos Bay, about 30 miles. Between Myrtle Point and Coquille is Johnson Mill Pond, a day-use area offering picnic tables, a fishing/swimming dock and short trails.

16. LaVerne Park – Moon Creek Tour

Road conditions: *Paved.*
Notes: *Roundtrip from Coos Bay to LaVerne County Park, 60 miles. Moon Creek loop adds about 20 miles. Good getaway from summer wind along coast. Camping, day-use, swimming, fishing.*

LaVerne Park is one of the crown jewels of the Coos County Parks system, and is actually two parks situated about 15 miles north of Co-quille. Tucked into a narrow canyon along the Coquille River's north fork, the park is well protected from the overcast, foggy or windy condi-tions that can prevail on the coast in summertime. Daytime tempera-tures can reach 80 and 90 degrees, making swimming and picnicking quite delightful.

West LaVerne Park caters to reserved picnics for up to 300 people, and there are large, covered shelters for such events, as well as horseshoe pits, two softball fields, playground area and trails. The main park offers camping and more group picnic areas with pavilions, another playground and ball field, and a swimming/wading area along a sandy beach.

It's all a nice drive, too. Beyond the park the road leads to paved roads through BLM land. You can make a loop out of part of the trek by continuing this way along Moon Creek. The forest roads are literally lined with wildflowers in summer, while in autumn you can enjoy the colorfully changing leaves of maples and other deciduous trees.

Getting There

From Coos Bay, head south on US 101 about 5 miles and take Highway 42 to Coquille. Take the West Coquille exit (West Central Blvd.), following signs to LaVerne Park. In 1 mile turn left on Fairview Rd., following signs to Fairview, LaVerne Park.

The road rolls through the lush pasturelands, passing peaceful country places. It weaves easily through the lowlands and begins a gentle climb into the hills, pushing up in earnest and topping off about 3.7 miles along. There are grand views to the east from here, miles of forest in various stages of growth, from recent clearcuts to older tracts.

Take it easy around the tight curves, then relax for the ride down toward Burton Prairie. About 7 miles from Coquille is Fairview and the "Four Corners" intersection with the Coos Bay Wagon Road (called Lone Pine Ln. along here). The store is last chance for provisions.

Proceed (N) across the intersection, still following signs to LaVerne Park, and passing many homey residences. The road follows the sinews of the Coquille River's north fork, choked by blackberry vine and brush.

If you're here in summer, the temperature rises delightfully in the sheltered canyons and small valleys, and the air is rich with birdsong and the smell of blossoms. A classic Smokey the Bear sign signals the end of "civilization" as the road plunges into the woods, and not far beyond is West LaVerne Park, where there's camping and group facilities.

The "main" park is just beyond, with camping, day-use, swimming and fishing. At this writing day-use was free.

Seeking sun, or shade? There are picnic tables and benches set about strategically for both. Other corners of the park offer places to play everything from volleyball to horseshoes, or you can just enjoy the farther reaches of cool serenity.

That vexing wind of the coast has been left far behind; it's mellowed to a gentle breeze that actually feels refreshing in the countrified heat, as does the river: wonderful and not cold at all.

Onward to Moon Creek

This, you might say, sounds like a fine enough outing. And you'd be correct. You could go to LaVerne Park, have a nice stay, turn around and come back. Why not? But for continued exploration, after a sojourn in LaVerne Park, press on (N) beyond the park.

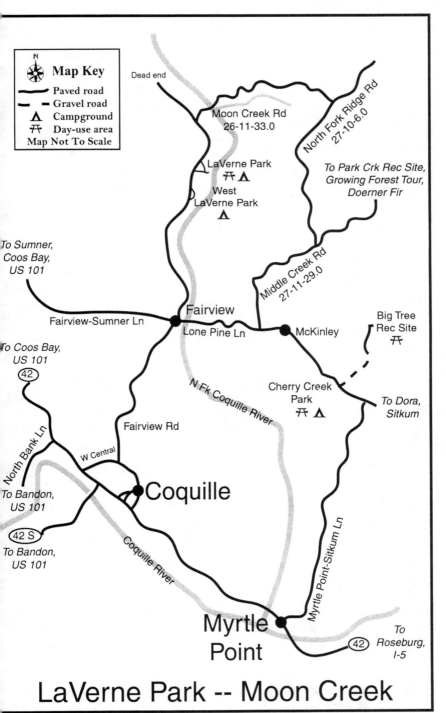

Map Key

— Paved road
- - Gravel road
△ Campground
⊼ Day-use area
Map Not To Scale

Dead end

Moon Creek Rd
26-11-33.0

North Fork Ridge Rd
27-10-6.0

To Park Crk Rec Site,
Growing Forest Tour,
Doerner Fir

LaVerne Park
⊼ △

West
LaVerne Park
△

To Sumner,
Coos Bay,
US 101

Middle Creek Rd
27-11-29.0

Fairview-Sumner Ln

Fairview

Lone Pine Ln

McKinley

Big Tree
Rec Site
⊼

To Coos Bay,
US 101

42

N Fk Coquille River

Cherry Creek
Park
⊼ △

To Dora,
Sitkum

Fairview Rd

North Bank Ln

W Central

Coquille

To Bandon,
US 101

42 S

To Bandon,
US 101

Coquille River

Myrtle Point-Sitkum Ln

Myrtle
Point

42

To
Roseburg,
I-5

LaVerne Park -- Moon Creek

In about 1.7 miles, turn right (E) on paved Moon Creek Rd., BLM 26-11-33.0 The road crosses a concrete bridge and heads east along Moon Creek, which flows through a picture-perfect corridor of sheltering alders. You're in serious wildflower country now, and the way during much of the summer is gloriously hemmed in with iris, tiger lilies, foxglove and many other varieties, along with such blooming shrubs as salmonberry and ocean spray.

After about 3.5 miles of level ambling through this wondrous forest, the road begins a gentle climb. The wildflowers now cascade off sheer hillsides, while succulent rockfasts burst forth in blossom from every nook and cranny. The climb becomes more pronounced as the road crosses the watershed divide.

Many intriguing-looking side roads intersect Moon Creek Rd., but stick to pavement. In about 7.4 miles from LaVerne Park is a "T" intersection with BLM 27-10-6.0. Turn right (S). The road heads downhill, offering views through the trees. Down, down we go!

At the bottom of the canyon, about 11.7 miles from LaVerne Park, is another "T" intersection, this one with BLM 27-11-29.0. This is Middle Creek Rd., although it's unmarked here except for a Growing Forest Tour sign. Turn right (S).The road follows Middle Creek, another pretty little stream bubbling through an arching canopy of white-barked alder. Here, too, are many huge moss-covered maples, their big leaves cool and green in summer and golden-hued in autumn.

A scattering of homes announces a gradual return from the deeper woods. More ranches and farms appear, and at about 20.7 miles from the start of this expedition at LaVerne Park is a "T" intersection with Lone Pine Ln. Turn right (W) and follow it about 5.3 miles back to Fairview, and from there turn left (S) to return to Coquille and Coos Bay.

17. The Big Trees — Forest Tour to Doerner Fir

Road conditions: *Paved except for 10-mile roundtrip on gravel access road to Doerner Fir. Year 'round access*
Notes: *About 120-mile roundtrip from Coos Bay. Camping, day-use, fishing. Best in late spring during wildflower and rhodie bloom, and in autumn for fall colors.*

The world's largest known coastal Douglas fir hides in the forests of Coos County, nestled in a classic stand of old-growth timber. Another huge tree ("The Forest Giant") stood a few canyons away until 1996, when it was felled by a root disease. The Forest Giant is still gigantic -- just on its side now -- and is set in a storybook picnic area surrounded by wondrously diverse woodlands.

Getting to these big trees is an adventure in itself. You'll spend the day on paved roads along ridgetops and canyons of spectacular forest, passing waterfalls and swimming holes, picnic and camping areas, wild-flowers and wildlife, a self-guided forest tour, and you'll have it practically all to yourself.

Generally referred to as the Tioga region, this area is a checkerboard divided up between timber corporations and the Bureau of Land Management (BLM), which has developed several recreation sites as well as a driving tour that takes you on a 60-mile loop through the woods.

A BLM guidebook to the Growing Forest Tour is available at their North Bend office and at visitor centers. The tour route is marked with distinctive "green tree" symbols.

Getting There

From Coos Bay, head south on US 101. At the "Y" about 5 miles south, take the left fork (Highway 42), following signs to Coquille, Roseburg. Continue another 14 miles to Coquille and take the West Coquille (West Central Blvd.) exit. Follow it 1 mile and turn left (N) on Fairview Rd., following signs to LaVerne Park, Fairview.

The lane ambles through the countryside, passing farms and ranches. It heads up and around some tight turns before dropping down to valley land and arriving in Fairview. There's a last-chance grocery here. You might also notice a sign for the Growing Forest tour.

At the Fairview intersection, turn right (E) on Lone Pine Lane (formerly called Coos Bay Wagon Road.) Head east, following signs to Dora, Sitkum and Middle Creek Rd. The route passes a power substation, crosses a concrete bridge, and heads up into the hills.

After ranging through the hills for a bit, the road drops down into a narrow valley, aiming for a tall stand of trees that marks the junction with Middle Creek Rd. About 5.3 miles from Fairview, turn left (N) on Middle Creek Rd., following signs to Burnt Mt. Access Rd., Park Creek recreation site and the Forest Tour.

The road heads up through a valley, past a handful of homesteads and ranches. About 5 miles up the canyon narrows, the river running right next to the road through columns of alder trees. The hillsides are thick with lush, almost luminous swordferns and undergrowth.

About 7 miles up, turn right (SE) at Burnt Mt. Access Rd., BLM 27-11-12.0, crossing a concrete bridge. Signs with the green-tree logo also point this way to the Growing Forest Tour. Up we go!

Spectacular overlooks await you along this ridgeline route, which is so neatly blacktopped and naturally "landscaped" that at times it seems like a private driveway to some mountaintop hideaway.

Before long you'll come to the first of six stops on the BLM driving tour. Most have short trails that end in cedar benches from which you can perch and contemplate the scenery.

If there's a flaw in the BLM's Growing Forest Tour, it's the fact that the forest has grown back! For example, the first stop was set amidst

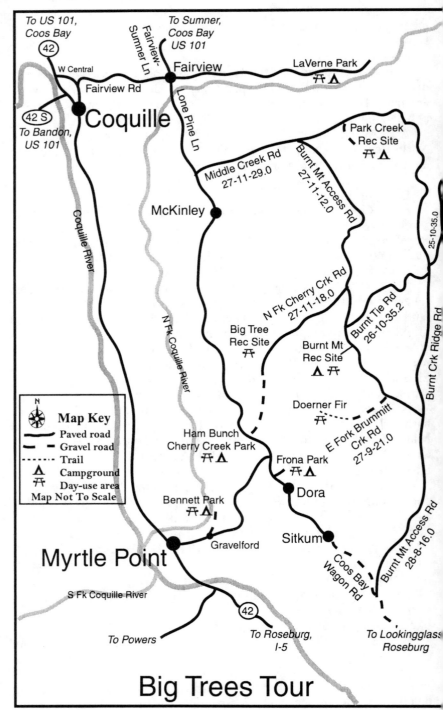

Big Trees Tour

a replanted clearcut, to show reforestation in its early stages. They're growing all right, so fast that this hardly looks like a "recent replant." The second, along a ridge in an area logged and replanted about 15 years ago, is thick with fir, alder, maple and myrtle trees, and dense underbrush.

A few miles from Stop 2 is a detour **not** in the BLM guidebook but which I highly recommend -- to the Big Tree recreation site. It's 4 miles down a paved road through huge old growth forest well worth a look. You'll have to backtrack out, but do make the effort.

Turn right (S) on No. Fork Cherry Creek Rd., BLM 27-11-18.0. The road heads down a canyon of aforementioned tall timber, and becoming the mainline Cherry Creek Rd.

The Big Tree site, 4 miles down, is as good as it gets, with little bridges and trails, and is home to what was until a few years ago the world's largest known Douglas fir. The discovery of a larger tree in a neighboring canyon didn't do much to diminish the grandeur of the Forest Giant, as it was called, but a disease called cubical butt rot did. Fearing that falling bark and limbs from the dying tree would crash down on visitors, the BLM cut the tree in 1996.

It was purposely felled upslope with minimal damage to adjacent trees, and left in place, and is still pretty impressive horizontally.

More tantalizing yet are the surrounding woodlands, a veritable library of diversity. Huge firs, cedars, hemlocks and deciduous trees -- we're not in a Douglas fir tree farm anymore! Take the footpath up the canyon; the earth here is so alive with robust growth of plants and trees it nearly *vibrates* . . .

Backtrack the way you came, up to the forest route on Burnt Mt. Access Rd. Turn right (E), and you'll soon come to Stop 3, a forest replanted in the '60s. Next is BLM Burnt Mt. recreation site, a day-use area and campground. (No water.) It's also Stop 4 on the forest tour.

About 4 miles east down the road from Burnt Mt. recreation site, turn right (S) on East Fork Brummitt Creek Rd., BLM 27-9-21.0. Tree-logo signs and directional signs indicate this as access to Doerner Fir. It's officially Stop 5 on the tour, down the only unpaved road on this trek (10 miles roundtrip).

Discovered in 1980 by an elk hunter and named after a retired forest administrator, the Doerner Fir is reached by a half-mile footpath through a cathedral of old growth. It soars up 329 feet — you can't even see the top from the base of the tree — and is nearly 12 feet in diameter.

Once back to Burnt Mt. Rd., turn left (W), back the way you came. Go back past the Burnt Mt. recreation site, to Burnt Tie Rd., BLM 26-10-35.2, and turn right (N), following the tree-logo signs.

The road drops quickly off the ridges, then loops down like a roller coaster to intersect Middle Creek Access Rd. Turn left (W).

The next landmark is BLM Park Creek recreation site, offering camp-

The Doerner Fir, largest known Coastal Douglas fir

ing and day-use (with water).

Continue down Middle Creek Rd, (passing the Burnt Mt. turnoff where this loop began) and return to the "T" intersection with Lone Pine Ln. Turn right (W), returning the way you came, following signs to Fairview. At Fairview, turn left (S), following signs to Coquille. Once back in Coquille at West Central Blvd., turn right (W) to return to Coos Bay.

PART TWO
THE POWERS REGION

The real secrets are up in the mountains. We know a bit about the beaches, and you've checked out a few back roads. Now it's time to get to the sweetness of the forest. Time to see the old growth trees, the rushing rivers, the soaring ridges.

Let's visit the often-overlooked Powers region. This northwest corner of the Siskiyou National Forest boasts wonders ranging from the botanical to the geological to the romantic.

The main route is officially called the Coquille-Rogue Scenic Byway, since it starts along the Coquille River's south fork and makes its way to the Rogue River. The Coquille-Rogue scenic byway is also a gateway to a few other equally memorable tours.

The first trip in this section describes the main route, about 185 miles if you make the whole loop from Coos Bay. That's a lot of driving even for a long summer day, especially on the many miles of twisting mountain and canyon roads. Consider a two-day trip, if possible.

Three other tours off the Powers-Agness Highway are described in subsequent chapters. The last chapter, Power(s) Walkin', deals with some hiking trails.

All routes and most trails are blocked by snow in winter. Flooding and landslides sometimes close roads for months. Barring those difficulties, you're in for scenic splendor. Officially designated and otherwise.

18. Lonely Rivers Flow — Coquille-Rogue Scenic Byway

Road conditions: *Paved except for 10-mile gravel section (pending pavement). Closed by snow in winter.*

Notes: *185-mile roundtrip from Coos Bay. Camping, day-use, hiking, fishing, swimming, boating. Wildflowers in late spring; showy colors in autumn. See Appendix A for information about Bald Knob Lookout and other lookout rentals*

The scenic byway portion of this tour begins along the Coquille River's south fork just outside Myrtle Point, and ends at US 101 in Gold Beach. You can make a loop by returning up US 101 to Coos Bay.

As noted earlier, this is an ambitious bit of driving for a single day, so consider turning it into an overnight, or longer, trip. There are many camping opportunities, and more "civilized" overnight accommodations along the Rogue River and in Gold Beach. You can even stay in forest fire lookout towers along the way, if you plan far enough ahead! There are dozens of potential stops at historic spots, fishing and swimming holes, vista points, lakes, rivers, waterfalls, big trees, hiking trails and bike tours. The route even has its own little guidebook, "Coastal Rivers Scenic Tour," available free from information centers and county, state and federal agencies.

Getting There

From Coos Bay, head south on US 101 about 5 miles to the "Y" junction and bear left on Highway 42, following signs to Coquille.

The road follows Isthmus Slough, one of the Coos Bay estuary's many inlets. There were pioneer-era coal mines and settlements at the far reaches of this slough, and small, ocean-going scows were loaded with ore bound for San Francisco. The highway sweeps past the settlement of Greenacres and climbs the rise that separates the Coos Bay estuary from Coquille Valley. This watershed divide reminded early settlers of the transit across the Isthmus of Panama, hence the name Isthmus Slough.

Next settlement is Coaledo, another one-time mining town.

After a few more wide turns through field and forest, you'll emerge on the Coquille Valley. It's all placid green pastureland in summer, but seasonal rains and high river levels turns this into a shimmering, shallow floodplain locals call Winter Lake.

Highway 42 bypasses Coquille and continues through the valley to Myrtle Point. About 3 miles beyond Myrtle Point, bear right (S), following signs to Powers. The route heads up through gently rolling hills, with the Coquille River's south fork bubbling by on your right.

Next is the settlement of Broadbent, founded in 1859 by a group from Baltimore, Md. They included doctors, craftsmen and tradesmen with a keen interest in farming and ranching, not to mention music and art. They grew everything from artichokes to bees to tobacco -- the latter is said to be Coos County's first commercial crop!

About 5 miles up is a rare sight, an old rusted "wigwam" burner at a small sawmill. It's a remnant of the old days in the Pacific Northwest when sawdust was burned to generate steam. It's no longer used, but you might see steam pouring from an adjacent building housing a boiler.

There are several places along the way officially designated for "angling access" for which you might notice signs. Some also have swimming opportunities, many complete with rope swing. The Powers Memorial Wayside is a grove of big myrtle trees, with access to the river. The road passes the settlement of Gaylord. Just beyond that is Coquille Myrtle Grove State Park, with picnic tables, restrooms and river access.

You'll pass neatly kept Century Farms and a few places not so well maintained. Some sport a half-dozen "No Trespassing" signs on the gates. Others welcome you to stop and purchase garlic or eggs or hay. You might glimpse exotic animals such as llamas, emus and albino deer on some of the spreads.

On the outskirts of Powers is the US Forest Service office, if you need to make inquiries or obtain maps and permits.

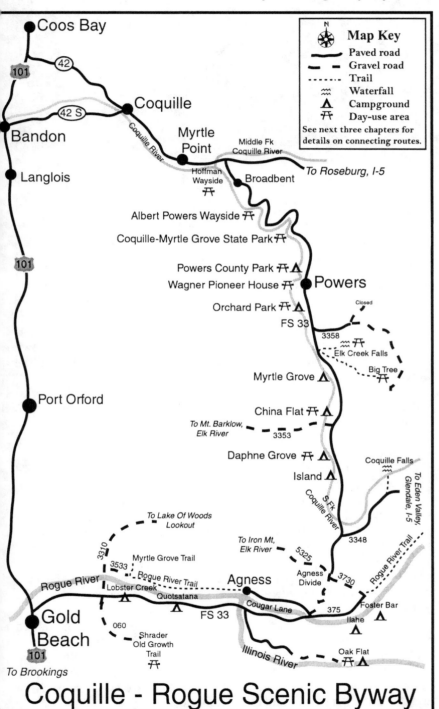

Map Key
- Paved road
- --- Gravel road
- ······ Trail
- ≈ Waterfall
- Δ Campground
- ⛨ Day-use area

See next three chapters for details on connecting routes.

Coos Bay

101 42

42 S

Coquille

Coquille River

Myrtle Point

Middle Fk Coquille River

Hoffman Wayside ⛨

Broadbent

To Roseburg, I-5

Langlois

Bandon

101

Albert Powers Wayside ⛨

Coquille-Myrtle Grove State Park ⛨

Powers County Park ⛨Δ

Wagner Pioneer House ⛨

Powers

Orchard Park ⛨Δ

FS 33

Closed

3358

≈⛨ Elk Creek Falls

Big Tree ⛨

Myrtle Grove Δ

Port Orford

China Flat ⛨Δ

To Mt. Barklow, Elk River

3353

Daphne Grove ⛨Δ

Coquille Falls ≈

Island Δ

Coquille River

S. Fk

To Eden Valley, Glendale, I-5

To Lake Of Woods Lookout

3310

To Iron Mt, Elk River

5325

3348

Rogue River Trail

3533

Myrtle Grove Trail

Rogue River Trail

Agness

Agness Divide

3730

Rogue River

Lobster Creek Δ

Quotsatana Δ

FS 33

Cougar Lane

375

Foster Bar Δ

Gold Beach

101

060

Shrader Old Growth Trail ⛨

Ilahe Δ

Illinois River

Oak Flat ⛨Δ

To Brookings

Coquille - Rogue Scenic Byway

Wagner Pioneer House is region's oldest residence

Just beyond is Powers County Park, with a 30-acre lake (formerly a mill pond), overnight camping and other amenities such as a playground and ball courts. Wheelchair accessible.

Powers itself is a classic little lumber town. Its isolation leads locals to joke Powers is "so far out in the middle of nowhere, the nearest town is called Remote." (Indeed, there's a settlement called Remote over the mountains to the northeast.)

First white settlers came from North Carolina, although in addition to indigenous people there were Chinese miners already in the vicinity. An early name was, appropriately enough, Rural.

The name eventually became Powers, after Albert Powers brought in a railroad in 1915 and set to work logging the surrounding mountains. This is another region of Coos County with a colorful history of rugged pioneer living, with many descendants of early settlers still around.

There are a few grocery stores, gas and auto repair and limited services. Right along the main road as it begins to zag through town is what's claimed to be the region's oldest dwelling, the Wagner Pioneer House. There's also a little railroad museum nearby, with some vintage equipment on display outside. Here also is a tiny building that once served as Gaylord's post office. The pioneer home and rail museum are open on the Fourth of July, when Powers celebrates its main event, White Cedar Days.

This once was a grand event in Powers, a celebration of the fabled Port Orford cedar tree and the people who worked in the woods, camps, mills and on the logging railroad. Folks came from throughout the region, and things sometimes got a bit lively, as might befit a logging town in the middle of nowhere. Celebrations in recent years are much more calm, and there's still a parade and other activities.

The rest of the year, don't expect a traffic jam.

Your transit on the main drag through Powers will include a swing to left, then right, following signs to China Flat, Ilahe, Agness. The road heads through the valley out of town and into the woods. A textbook transition.

About 4 miles from town is the Siskiyou National Forest boundary, and the canyon narrows as it follows the sinews of the Coquille River's south fork. The route becomes FS 33, and there are occasional turnouts for river access.

About 5 miles out you'll pass FS 3358, a side road to the USFS Big Tree recreation site, home of the world's largest Port Orford cedar. It's 4.2 miles up a rough road that has sections of pavement, gravel and dirt. The cedar sits on a slope amidst other big trees of several species. There's also a trail to the Big Cedar, which starts from Elk Creek Falls (just ahead). For information about the Big Cedar, see chapter 21, Big Cedar Trail.

Not far from the FS 3358 along FS 33 is the trail to Elk Creek Falls. Park along the road and follow the short but lovely trail through lush ferns and tall trees to the falls. There are shady picnic tables and benches. Summer and autumn find the water lacing down in a delicate tracery of mist and water; winter and spring flows are more robust. Study the cliffs below the falls for hanging gardens of ferns and moss, and watch for tiny birds flitting through the spray.

The trail is cool green grotto in summer, but particularly wondrous in autumn, when huge maple leaves lie like oversized orange stepping stones along the path.

Also at the Elk Creek Falls parking area is a trail up to the world's largest known Port Orford cedar tree. It's a challenging hike; see chapter 21 for details.

Back on the road, you'll next encounter USFS Myrtle Grove campground, offering river access and primitive camping.

Just beyond is China Flat, where Georgia-Pacific has an undeveloped camping area. There's access to a wide, gravely part of the river here. To the right (W) is FS 3353 to Butler Bar, Elk River, US 101. (For details on this route, see chapter 23.)

The name China Flat derives from a late-1800s encampment of Chinese gold miners. According to a historical essay by Powers resident Gladys Tanner, white settlers were "uneasy with the Chinese, who were very superstitious, so it was an easy task to scare them out." The settlers launched nighttime forays against the Chinese, who eventually left. In a telling afternote, she says "the settlers could not get along nearly as well with the Chinese gone as they did while they were here."

Across the river is the Port Orford Cedar Research Area. Also called white cedar or Lawson cypress, the trees have an instantly-recognizable aroma some liken to ginger, and possesses remarkably resilient

Elk Creek Falls is a highlight of the Coquille - Rogue Byway

properties. The long thread-like fibers resist rot and decay, and the wood has been used for everything from heavy industrial applications to fenceposts to finely finished wood pieces. It even resists acid, and has been used for battery separators.

Its light, satiny texture when finished makes it popular for use as indoor trim, and it's especially prized in Japan because it resembles the nearly extinct hinoki cypress, used for icon pieces in shrines. Like its red and yellow cedar cousins, white cedar was used by Indians for shelter, baskets, canoes, even clothing.

Unfortunately, Port Orford cedars have been attacked by a root fungus that threatens to wipe them out. Research is under way in this area and other parts of the region to save Port Orford cedar. Efforts include experimental plantings of disease-resistant trees.

The root disease is spread by spores that travel in water and mud, so special restrictions apply on roads leading from infected regions to so-far healthy stands. The tires of logging trucks and other vehicles must be washed before leaving contaminated areas. There are stands of uninfected Port Orford cedars, but it's uncertain whether the species will survive, so it's important to obey travel restrictions and follow any other rules that will help save this unique tree. The spores that kill cedars are also blamed for a late-20th century disease that has decimated California's oaks, and is attacking other trees, too. (See appendix B for more information.)

There's no official trail or access to the Port Orford Cedar Research Area, but you can wander amidst the trees and see a house sheathed in its bark. The house is being restored by the Forest Service. Look for a road about 3 miles beyond China Flat. It crosses a bridge over the river and is gated off, so you'll have to park and walk. The bark-covered house is about a half-mile down the road.

The USFS Daphne Grove campground comes next, where amenities include potable but coppery-tasting water, as well as day-use and river access. Up the road less than two miles is USFS Island campground, and a few bends in the road beyond is a roadside interpretive and picnic area. The road crosses a bridge; say goodbye to the south fork of the Coquille River.

Around the bend is FS 3348, to Coquille Falls, Eden Valley, Mt. Bolivar and Glendale. (See chapters 19 & 20.)

The route follows Rock Creek now; you'll pass FS 3347 to USFS Rock Creek campground.

And now the final climb, up what seems like the back of some gigantic creature. They've left a few groves of big old trees up here — who knows for how long — to add drama to the climb. You'll pass gravel roads from the left, and if you crane your neck up in that direction you can spot Bald Knob lookout tower. And then you're at the top.

Stop and take in the view. This is called Agness Pass, but it has the feeling of an ancient crossroads. Higher ridges loom up to the east and west; you've slipped through a saddle, or low point, in the range. This is the watershed divide between the Coquille and Rogue rivers, as well as the Coos-Curry county line; maybe it was once a tribal boundary or ceremonial spot?

Gravel roads head off to the left and right, and behind you is the rugged terrain you've just traversed. Ahead is a dreamy, seemingly endless sea of trees, with a glimpse of the Rogue River far below.

Continue south on FS 33, which turns to gravel for the next 9 miles. (It's a slight departure from the official scenic byway; a shorter, safer way down. It's scheduled to be paved, and may be so as you read this.)

These are drier, southern-exposure slopes, home to such sun-loving trees as madrone, with its distinctive peeling bark and red "skin" underneath. Tanoak and manzanita grow in abundance, as does poison oak.

The road loops down and down. Take it easy on the gravel! Twice you'll pass spurs to Lake Of the Woods, but stick to the main route. (Lake Of the Woods, by the way, is a tiny, seasonal pond that dries out in summer.)

Pavement returns as you reach the bottom near the Rogue River. Just before the crossing is an intersection, with the upriver road heading to Ilahe and Foster Bar (about 3 miles), and the downriver route leading to Agness (also 3 miles). The main route crosses the river and continues down to Gold Beach.

Ilahe, Foster Bar and a dayhike on the upper Rogue River Trail

There's a USFS campground at Ilahe (Indian word for "land"). It offers drinking water, and is on the grounds of an early homestead. Nearby is historic Santa Anita Lodge (also known as Ilahe Lodge), one of several rustic inns along the Rogue River that offer lodging and meals.

There's a boat launch at Foster Bar, and swimming spots. Use caution in the Rogue; its current is powerful. Also be alert for powerful jet boats plying the river; their wake can swamp smaller craft and wash away toddlers, animals and belongings.

Near Foster Bar is a trailhead for backpacking entry into the Rogue River Wilderness Area. It's a rugged 15 miles to Marial, but for a good day-hike, consider the 9-mile-roundtrip up to Flora Dell Falls. You'll cross old pastures and gentle slopes above the river — and five streams — before reaching the falls and its pool, the latter into which you can plunge into for a rewarding swim.

Agness and a dayhike on the lower Rogue River Trail

The side road down to Agness is another single-lane (but paved) route just above the river. After a couple of miles you'll pass the Singing Springs Resort (food and lodging) on the left. The resort is also a stop for one of the commercial jet boat outfits, so you might notice groups of people coming and going. Nearby is the Agness museum, open seasonally. Next is the Agness store, with basic supplies. The road continues south past the store and turns to gravel and dirt as it heads down to a gravel bar along the river. There's primitive camping here, and swimming and fishing.

A right (W) turn on Cougar Ln. at the store leads past Lucas Lodge (a family-style restaurant), ending near Agness school and library. Here

Shady picnic retreat along the Coquille - Rogue Byway

is the trailhead for the lower portion of the Rogue River Trail.

The parking area for the trail is just past the school. Park and walk down the rest of the gravel road, past private residences, to find the trailhead. This section of trail is a difficult 12-plus miles, but you can again take a little jaunt to get a feel for the place.

Best bet for this is the 6.5-mile roundtrip to Painted Rock Creek, which includes a stop at Big Eddy and a look at the Rogue's famed

Copper Canyon. Follow the trail about 1 mile and take the left fork to reach Big Eddy, the only practical river access on this hike.

Backtrack to the main hiking trail and follow the right fork. You'll cross several streams on the way up to the promontory above Copper Canyon, where in addition to a classic river view you can enjoy the delicate wildflowers and lichen eking out an existence on rock outcrops.

If you want to go on a bit, continue 0.5 mile to Painted Rock Creek, where a waterfall hides amidst the ferns and mossy rocks. Indian pictographs were found on the rocks near the mouth of the creek.

Cougar Lane to Gold Beach

Continuing on the main route (FS 33) at the Agness turnoff, cross the bridge and turn right (S). You'll have a clear view of the mighty Rogue, whose name is yet another source of historic conjecture. Some theories say trouble between local Indians and early French explorers and trappers led the French to call them *les coquins,* which Englishmen correctly translated as "the rogues."

The troubles between whites and Indians led to the so-called Rogue River Indian Wars, which lasted until 1855 and involved bloody battles and massacres. Only about 1,200 Indians remained by the time they were overwhelmed and forcibly taken to a reservation up the coast.

The road continues above the river, passing the Shasta-Costa riffle and a couple of USFS roads to the east. About 3 miles of travel along this side of the river will bring you to Cougar Lane Resort, with general store, gas pumps, restaurant, motel and a campground that offers a gravel bar for fishing, swimming and boat launching. One of the commercial jet boat outfits stops here -- the other stops directly across the river at Singing Springs Resort -- so the roar of boats is a common sound.

Past Cougar Lane the road encounters a soaring span over the Illinois River at its confluence with Rogue River. The nationally-designated Wild and Scenic Illinois River is another emerald ribbon of wonder, although wide and pretty tame here.

Just before the bridge is the way to Oak Flat (3 miles, including some bad pot-holes), with primitive camping, swimming opportunities, a wooden picnic overlook, and a take-out point for Illinois River rafters.

Just across the bridge is a hiking trail to the east that offers a little taste of the terrain along the Illinois River, but no river access.

The main road loses sight of the Rogue River at times, with no access for many miles. The road is paved but built on constantly-settling earth so there are lots of cracks and rough spots. There are a couple of campgrounds with river access as you get nearer to Gold Beach, and a couple of hiking opportunities.

USFS Quosatana campground is 15 miles downriver from Cougar Lane (13 miles upriver from Gold Beach). USFS Lobster Creek campground is 18 miles downriver from Cougar Lane (10 miles upriver from

Gold Beach.) Across the road from Lobster Creek campground is Kimball Hill Rd., FS 060, which leads in 2 miles to the Shrader Old Growth Trail, a 1-mile walk through giant firs and cedars.

Just over the bridge at Lobster Creek is another grove of huge trees, this time myrtlewood. Take the first right just north of the bridge to have a look at the Myrtle Grove Trail, and if you're feeling inspired by the heady perfume of the huge leafy trees, scramble up the trail above the access road.

It's another 10 miles downriver from Lobster Creek to Gold Beach. You'll emerge on US 101 just south of the distinctive bridge over the river. Turn left to enter Gold Beach, or turn right to return to Coos Bay (75 miles). More details about locales on the way back can be found in chapters 3, 4 and 20.

19. Headin' Out to Eden -- Mt Bolivar Tour

Road conditions: *Paved. Closed by snow in winter.*
Notes: *Coos Bay to Mt. Bolivar and back — 240 miles roundtrip. Entire tour via Riddle with return on Highway 42 — 265 miles. Camping, swimming, fishing. Designated bike route.*

Here's a tour along a remote backcountry byway to Mt. Bolivar, Coos County's highest peak, with the potential to continue on paved roads to Interstate 5 and return to Coos Bay via Highway 42. If you're not up for the whole loop, consider stopping at some of the sites along the way and cap off the tour with a hike up Mt. Bolivar, then return the way you came. It's scenic even if you do it twice!

In spring and early summer the forests burst with wildflowers and rhodies in bloom. As summer progresses the leafy maples and alders provide a natural awning of cool relief, while the river tempts with dozens of swimming holes. Autumn is the most dramatic. Gigantic leaves waft from the big old maples, and the alders shiver their golden mantles, just part of the colorful show.

The Powers-Glendale road is an officially-designated backcountry bicycle route. Note for bicyclists: The tour described here will leave the bike route a few miles outside Glendale, opting for a return to I-5 at Riddle. The map shows both routes.

Getting There
Proceed to Powers on the Coquille-Rogue Scenic Byway as discussed in the previous chapter. From Powers, continue south, following signs to China Flat, Ilahe, Agness; 4 miles from Powers the route becomes FS 33. See the preceding chapter for details on Elk Creek Falls, campgrounds and other stops along the way.

If there's a drawback to this route, it's the lack of potable drinking

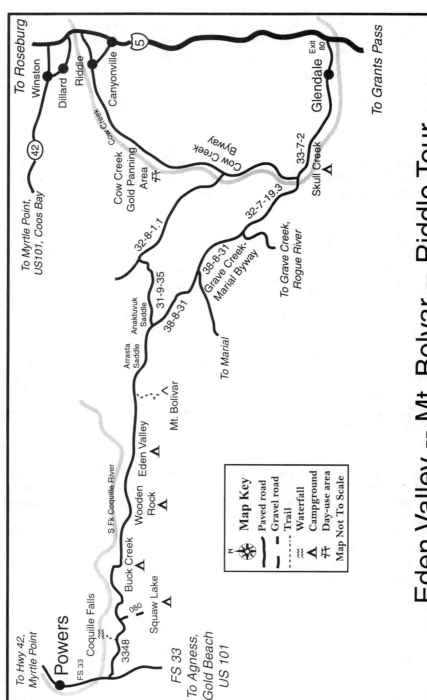

Eden Valley -- Mt. Bolvar -- Riddle Tour

water. The USFS Daphne Grove campground, about 14.5 miles out of Powers on FS 33, is the last opportunity for many miles.

17 miles past Powers, turn left (E) on FS 3348, following signs to Eden Valley and Glendale. The lane climbs up into steep, old growth forest.

In 1.5 miles is Coquille Falls Natural Area, with a trail down to Coquille Falls. (See chapter 21.)

Continue on FS 3348, following signs to Glendale. Little waterfalls pour forth from the thickly forested slopes above the road, feeding the bubbling river on the other side.

You'll pass FS 080 to Squaw Lake, where there's a USFS campground. There are other USFS campsites and campgrounds as the route heads into Eden Valley. The valley sits at the base of a long, east-west running escarpment called Eden Ridge, which in addition to yielding a bonanza of timber in the early years, is rich with coal. Pioneer mines tapped some of the seams, and to this day there's occasional interest in further mining. The timber has been and continues to be harvested, and many slopes are in various stages of regrowth.

Just east of the USFS Eden Valley campground are three interpretive signs that describe the early-day settlement here, which included two sawmills and a rail line. As for the name *Eden*, historians suggest only the obvious: original settlers thought this was "as good as it gets." With settlers long gone, there's a palpable sense of isolation in this little mountain valley.

The byway heads uphill, with panoramas opening eastward. You'll enter BLM land; the road changes to BLM 32-8-3.1 (Kelsey Mule Rd.) Not far beyond is a parking area for the Mt. Bolivar Trail.

Mt. Bolivar Trail: At 4,319 feet, this is the highest peak in the Coast Range north of the Rogue River, but the trail is a lark compared with some of the others in the vicinity (described in chapter 17). Switchbacks soften a gradual ascent, and sections of deep woods and rock-bound "gardens" of tiny succulents enliven the climb. And that view!

Mt. Bolivar Trail (FS 1259) is 1.4 miles to the top, ambling up from the trailhead through big manzanitas, wild rhodies and spindly pines. You can see the mountaintop up to the left, a gentle dome, nothing scary. The footpath heads into the woods, looping up and around to the mountain's rocky north flanks. Hardy succulents and wildflowers grow amidst the rocks, which themselves support colonies of lichen and mosses.

The trail continues up the stony slopes to the mountaintop, rock-strewn home to a few trees that tell a tale of relentless wind and weather.

Mt. Bolivar is in the unique position of straddling three watersheds: the Rogue River to the south, Coquille River to the north, and Cow Creek (an Umpqua River tributary) to the east. Which way does a waterdrop roll from here?

You can easily spot snow-capped Mt. McLoughlin off to the south-

Wild rhododendrons bloom along easy trail up Mt. Bolivar

east, and on a clear day pick out distant Cascade Mountain peaks. To the north is the distinctive east-west escarpment of Eden Ridge and the meadowy greens of its valley.

South are hundreds of square miles of the rugged, plunging jumble of Coast Range and Siskiyou mountains, while immediately west are Diamond Peak and the aptly-named Saddle Peaks, a sharp ridgeline with three connected high points. That rare day clear of fog, haze or forest fire smoke may bring a glimpse of the ocean.

From up here, as the old-timers said, you can see and see and see.

The footings of a former lookout are evident, and there's a plaque from the people of Venezuela, a goodwill gesture by foreign exchange and local students in the 1980s.

Mt. Bolivar is said to have been named in honor of South American liberator Simon Bolivar, although it was named by Coos County's first surveyor, who happened to be named Simon Bolivar Cathcart.

Continuing on the road past Mt. Bolivar, the route rolls just below a ridgeline through fine old trees surrounded by wild rhodies. Big vistas eastward!

You'll pass other roads, but stick to BLM 32-8-31, following a sign to Grave Creek. The road tops out about 2 miles past Mt. Bolivar. This is Arrasta Saddle, at 3,256 feet the high point of the drive, with restrooms placed as part of the bikeway development. About 1 mile beyond is a major pass called Anaktuvuk Saddle.

Veering slightly southwest, continue on the main road (BLM 32-8-31), passing two roads (BLM 32-9-16.2 and 16.1) to the left and two to the right (BLM 32-19-16 and an unnumbered road).

Just beyond is another fork in the road, this one marked by signs. Take the right fork, (BLM 32-8-31) following the sign to Cold Springs Camp, Tucker Flat, Marial, Glendale, Grants Pass.

2 miles beyond is Bobby Saddle, with a water hole for tanker trucks and a memorial plaque for a firefighter lost in the line of duty.

Keep on BLM 32-8-31 at the next intersection, following a sign to Grave Creek. You'll intercept Grave Creek-Marial Backcountry Byway (BLM 32-9-14.2); turn SE and get on it and follow signs to Grants Pass and Grave Creek.

In just 0.1 mile, go left on Bobby Creek Rd., BLM 32-8-9.2. The road heads down, passing a stand of madrone trees. Then, here we go! Down and down and around and around, at one point passing a fenced-off "progeny" plantation, where seedling trees from different breeding stock are studied for growth and health characteristics. You'll get glimpses of water flashing down in the canyon; after about 4 miles the road finally gets to the west fork of Cow Creek. Cross the bridge over the creek and follow the road up to a "T" intersection.

Turn right on BLM 32-8-1.1, following the sparkling creek. You'll pick up double-yellow and fog lines after about 1 mile, and in a couple more is the main stem of Cow Creek. Go across the railroad tracks and a bridge to a "T" intersection.

Turn left (N) on Cow Creek Rd. and follow it along the river. (Powers-Glendale Bike Route note: turn right to continue to Glendale, I-5.)

Except for the railroad on the other side, the landscape is wild and undeveloped. In about 3 miles is a BLM recreational gold panning area. Gold in Cow Creek tantalized settlers as early as 1853, but panning it was difficult. "We found potholes (with) fine, light gold," wrote settler Herman Reinhart. "But it was hard to save, for the sand was nearly as heavy as the gold. It took great care and still you could see the gold wash out of the pan and lodge on a rock down the stream."

A bit beyond the gold panning area are the fascinating rocks and outcrops of Iron Mountain. Flying saucers, anyone?

A few homesteads signal the beginning of human settlement again. There's a Historic Place in the form of a collapsed Oregon & California Line railroad tunnel.

Next landmark is the hulking slag heap at Glenbrook Nickel smelter. This was the first major nickel mine in the U.S., with work commencing in 1882. The smelter later took in nickel from other parts of the world, smelting it into ferronickel ingots, or "pigs." Among other things, nickel is used in the manufacture of stainless steel, so a lot of the pigs were shipped to Midwest steel plants. In recent times the plant has been shut down, owing to a worldwide downturn in the value of nickel ore.

Follow the main road into Riddle and from there connect with I-5. To return to Coos Bay (about 100 miles), head north on I-5 for 10.5 miles to exit 112, following signs to Coos Bay.

The route passes the Roseburg Lumber Co. mill near Dillard, one of the largest sawmills in the Pacific Northwest, and continues to Winston, where you can pick up Highway 42 to the coast. Under normal conditions the trip back to Coos Bay takes about two hours.

(For more information about Highway 42, see chapter 13.)

20. A Sea of Rhodies: Panther Ridge to Hanging Rock

Road conditions: *Paved and gravel. Closed by snow in winter.*
Notes: *150-mile roundtrip from Coos Bay. Best in early June for rhododendron bloom. See Appendix A for information about Bald Knob Lookout and other lookout rentals.*

Here's another excursion in the Powers region of the Siskiyou National Forest, up into the higher reaches and ridges above Eden Valley, along the edge of the Wild Rogue Wilderness Area.

Getting there will take you through some beautiful forest scenery, and you can stop for a picnic, swim or short hike at many places along

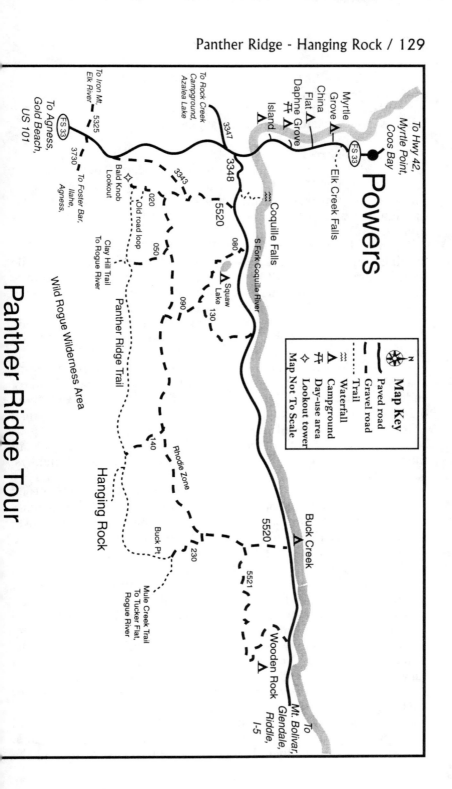

Panther Ridge Tour

the way. Our destination is Hanging Rock, sometimes called Coos County's "geologic wonder." The promontory is along 7.2-mile Panther Ridge Trail, which has four access points. We'll be heading for the trailhead that's about 1 mile from Hanging Rock.

Getting There

Proceed to Powers on the Coquille-Rogue Scenic Highway as discussed in chapter 18. That chapter has info on sights along the way. From Powers, stay on the main road as it doglegs through town, following signs to China Flat, Ilahe, Agness. The route becomes FS 33 about 4 miles from Powers.

17 miles from Powers, turn left (E) on FS 3348. It cuts immediately uphill through majestic old growth forest. 1.5 miles up is the Coquille Falls Natural Area. Refer to the previous chapter for details. 0.5 mile beyond, just past a MP 2 marker, turn right (W) on FS 5520, following signs to Bald Knob Lookout and Panther Ridge Trail.

The gravel road heads uphill along forested slopes, then turns south. In about 1 mile, just past FS 3343, is FS 020, the road to Bald Knob Lookout and the western terminus of Panther Ridge Trail, 3 miles.

(*FS 020/Bald Knob Lookout/Panther Ridge Trail western terminus notes*: The public-access part of FS 020 proceeds about 3 miles, ending at a gate near the Panther Ridge Trail (FS 1253) trailhead, about 0.25 mile from the lookout tower. Bald Knob Lookout is a seasonal USFS rental; for more info about lookout rentals, see Appendix B.)

The western end of Panther Ridge Trail begins in a stand of tall timber thick with downed wood in some places and lined with rhodies, ferns, salal, and wildflowers in others. A curious mix!

Continuing on FS 5520, the road continues past the turnoff to Bald Knob Lookout, and in about 1.6 miles encounters FS 050, second access to Panther Ridge Trail. This road heads uphill through regrowth forest and a thick rhodie zone for about 1 mile to the trailhead. If intact, signs mark the trail, and there's a map and information.

Continuing on FS 5520, you'll pass many side roads, and traverse a veritable sea of rhodies. It's said this is one of the most intense stands of wild rhododendrons in the Siskiyou National Forest. In about 3 miles, turn right on FS 140, following a sign to Panther Ridge Trail. The trailhead is about 1 mile, (again amidst a sea of wild rhodies), with signs and info.

As noted, this is the shortest way to Hanging Rock. Park at the trailhead, secure your vehicle and follow the trail (FS 1253-A) up an easy slope of rhodies and salal to the crossroads with the main trail (FS 1253). Turn left, and after a short uphill, then downhill stretch, watch for the Hanging Rock Trail (1253-A) to the right.

Follow the path for about 10 minutes; you'll come to a post in the trail and some rocky outcrops, but keep going; a bit ahead is mightier drama: Hanging Rock -- and it literally is -- with a view all the way through the

Hanging Rock overlooks the Wild Rogue Wilderness

Wild Rogue Wilderness and beyond. Look down – and down and down – and you can spot the Rogue River glinting through the trees. Turkey vultures and eagles may be soaring down in the canyon, but don't be surprised if they spot you and float up for a closer look!

The views, the silence, the sighing of the trees make this a hard place to leave. But when you're ready, retrace your route from Hanging Rock, making sure not to miss the side trail (1253-A) to the parking area!

Back in your vehicle, retrace your route back at FS 5520, turn right, and in about 6 miles you'll come to the fourth access road, FS 230, to the Panther Ridge Trail and Buck Point. This would be the 7.2-mile trail's eastern terminus; here too are connections with Wild Rogue Wilderness trails. It's a rough 0.8-mile track, cut with waterbars, and the views at the top aren't nearly as noteworthy as from Hanging Rock, so I don't recommend it unless you're launching a hike.

Continue on FS 5520 to its intersection with the Eden-Glendale route, FS 3348, and turn left (W), following the sign to Powers, 26 miles. Directly across the way is USFS Buck Creek campground. Heading west, FS 3348 sweeps through primeval forestland, with the Coquille River's south fork tumbling along to the right. In a handful of miles you'll pass the turn where this loop started. Continue down the canyon and turn right (N) on FS 33 to return to Powers.

21. Powers Walkin' — Six short hikes in the Powers area

Road conditions: *Paved- and gravel-road access to trails, which are steep and challenging. Subject to snow-time closure.*
Notes: *Rugged, steep trails for hikers in proper condition.*

In the vicinity of Powers are a handful of trails that rival any piece of exercise equipment. No need for the treadmill, these trails give a workout to everything you've got. Oh, you'll feel the burn, all right. We be Powers Walkin.'

For all these hikes, proceed to Powers on the Coquille-Rogue Scenic Byway as discussed in chapter 14. Continue on the main road through Powers, following signs to China Flat, Ilahe, Agness. About 4 miles out of Powers, the route becomes FS 33.

1. Coquille Falls: We'll start with the easiest one, the 0.5-mile trail down to the staircase waterfalls in the Coquille Falls Natural Area. The falls hide in a canyon of towering old growth forest, and the upper cascade offers a pool for swimming and lots of rocks for sunning. Getting down is a snap, but make the effort to stop and soak in the scenery, because when you're climbing back up you won't be quite so jolly.

Depending on your conditioning, it takes about 10 minutes to walk down and a good half-hour to get back up.

Getting There

From Powers, follow FS 33 about 17 miles and turn left (E) on FS 3348, following signs to Eden Valley and Glendale. The road twists uphill through a forest of imposing specimens. About a 1 mile from the turn, you'll cross a bridge over a stream. About 0.5 mile beyond is the pullout for Coquille Falls Trail, FS 1257.

This trail doesn't waste any time, pitching immediately downhill through the woods. But what a forest! A veritable library of trees, including grand old fir, cedar, spruce and hemlock, among others.

The stately silence of the ancient forest is broken before long by a roaring from the gorge, and through the trees below you might catch a glint of sunlight off the falls.

The footpath makes a few switchbacks to ease the hike, but you'll have to hold the reins to keep from pitching quickly downward. You'll encounter a trickling watercourse called Drowned-Out Creek, then cross it near the bottom of the canyon.

There's a rough trail to the upper falls here, but proceed downhill to the lower falls viewpoint. Twin cascades of water carve through siltstone bluffs, often framed in a rainbow mist. You can scramble up the rocks to the upper pool, but be *extremely careful*.

The upper pool has a picturebook lagoon for swimming, surrounded by wide, flat rock ledges.

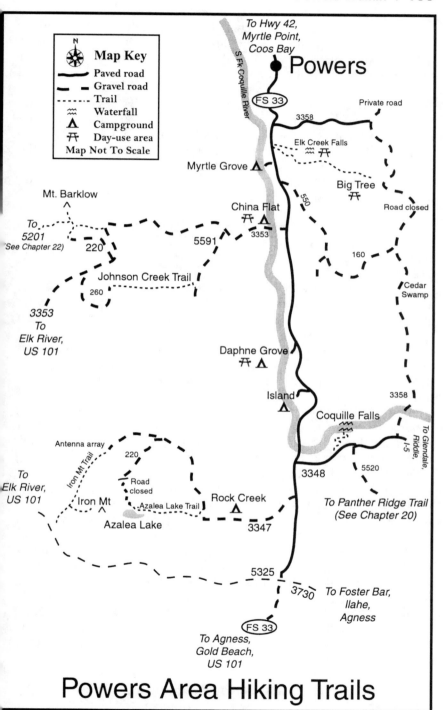

Powers Area Hiking Trails

As if the place weren't nice enough, you're made even more reluctant to leave when pondering that hike out. Just remember to take it slowly. Take frequent breaks. You'll be back on top and in the car again soon enough, what's the rush?

2. Big Cedar: You can actually drive to the Big Tree recreation site, home of the world's largest Port Orford cedar, or you can get to it on a 1.2 mile trail that begins near Elk Creek Falls, along FS 33.

This is the epitome of Powers Walkin', a relentless push UP the spine of a ridge, nary a switchback the whole way. Then some *more* uphill and then a last push uphill to the big tree, which sits amidst many other fine old specimens of trees.

Getting There

A bit over 5 miles from Powers on FS 33 is the parking area and trailhead for the Elk Creek Falls Trail and Big Cedar Trail. Have a look at the falls for inspiration, then locate the adjacent trail (FS 1150) to the Big Cedar.

The first 10 minutes are intensely vertical, up through huge old growth along the backbone of a ridge. Topping out a bit, the way passes under aromatic myrtlewood trees, around a huge uprooted trunk and through a garden of wild rhodies.

There's a brief downhill stretch, with the trail paralleling an old logging track. The trail merges with the logging road. In a couple of hundred feet, look for a path to the left that leads to the Big Cedar. A hiking trail directional sign if intact points the way.

This last stretch of trail goes through a glade of big old trees, each covered with a thick coat of moss. There's a sort of reverential hush, or maybe the moss just absorbs all the sound, but it's really nice through here. The trail comes to a junction with the path from the parking area. There's a picnic table tucked off to the right.

Turn left at the junction and continue to the Big Cedar overlook.

The Big Cedar, 239 feet tall and 12.4 feet in diameter, is hard to spot until you're upon it, since it sits among equally large companions. They include an Oregon Grand fir, the only true fir found at sea level in the state. (The better-known and widely-farmed Douglas fir is actually a type of hemlock; it's hardier than the Grand fir, which is susceptible to Indian paint fungus. Grand fir can be distinguished by needles of unequal length.)

The hike up the grove, a good hour or more, takes only about 30 minutes on the return, and quickly makes you forget the work involved in the climb up. *Now* your only worry is to keep from pitching headlong downhill . . .

3. Azalea Lake: Of all the mudponds loftily called "lakes" in this region, Azalea is one of the few worthy of the name. Good thing, too,

Old raft on Azalea Lake brings out the Huck Finn in everyone

since getting to it is uphill all the way. The trail is just 1.2 miles long, mercifully.

It deserves the effort, as it's surrounded, appropriately enough, by wild azaleas and rhododendrons that bloom vigorously in June and July. The clear water warms up enough for swimming, and there are nice picnic spots.

Getting There

From Powers, follow FS 33 about 17.5 miles past Powers and turn right (W) on FS 3347, following signs to USFS Rock Creek campground. The campground comes along in about 1 mile.

Continue past the campground on FS 3347. Just over a bridge across Rock Creek, the road encounters a "Y" intersection with an adjacent parking area for the Azalea Lake Trail (FS 1262).

The trail follows an old jeep track; as noted it's a vertical incline all the way, about 1 mile.

Once at the lake, the nicest spots are at the west end near the trail, but by exploring the path around the lake you'll find other places, too.

4. Barklow Mountain: Another challenging route, with three different approaches to a peak that overlooks Coast Range terrain clear to the sea. A fire lookout once stood atop Barklow Mountain, named for a pioneer family. You can get to the trail from FS 3353, a gravel road off the main route, FS 33. There's another trailhead along FS 5201, described in chapter 22.

The eastside slopes are covered in sizeable timber, and thick with wild rhodies. The summit and western flanks are the perfect habitat for manzanita. It blooms for a long time in late winter and early spring, attracting bees that help the plant to set tiny fruit -- hence the name, which is Spanish for little apples.

Getting There

Proceed from Powers on what becomes FS 33 and in 9 miles turn right (W) at China Flat on gravel FS 3353, following signs to Mt. Barklow Trail, Butler Bar, Elk River, US 101. See the following chapter for details of the entire route.

11 miles up is a parking area for Mt. Barklow Trail, FS 1258. Best described as a goat-path, the trail heads up a flank of the mountain. There are only a few switchbacks, but the trail passes under some outstanding old-growth fir.

Once at the ridgeline, turn right and trek the remaining uphill section to the top. There's a side trail down to another trailhead (described next), as well as a trail to the old lookout cabin and FS 5201 (see chapter 22).

The wild rhodies grow -- and bloom in early June -- all the way along, right to the peak.

No trace remains of the fire lookout, which was helicoptered over to Lake Of the Woods Mnt. above Rogue River. In recent years the trees have been growing up to obscure views north and east, but on a clear day you can easily see the ocean, about 20 miles distant.

Option #2 from FS 3353: Continue past Mt. Barklow Trail parking area and turn right on FS 220, a rugged dirt road that in 3.7 miles ends at a trailhead on Mt. Barklow's south side. The trail begins on the northwest corner of the parking area. The footpath heads up through thick manzanita, salal and Oregon grape, intercepting the main track, which continues northwest up the ridgeline. You'll pass the trail to the lookout cabin on this route.

(The cabin, about 0.3 mile down the trail, is a deteriorating wooden-frame shelter set amidst tall firs. Not very charming; mainly of interest for its historical significance.)

5. Johnson Creek Trail: This is 2.4 miles up (or down, depending on where you start) through a canyon of old-growth timber, ranging well above what is actually Sucker Creek. Once a route for early-day miners, it's one of the few trails in the Powers Ranger District that didn't get turned into a road. The trail's lower end begins near the confluence of Johnson and Sucker creeks, and the latter must be forded to commence the hike. It's a tricky crossing, unsafe in high water times. The trail's upper end begins off a sideroad of FS 3353 (China Flat-Elk River route), not far from Mt. Barklow Trail. The path crosses a number of tiny creeks, and there's a campsite in a level, shady patch of ground, but otherwise this is pretty much a narrow path down a canyon, with few places to get near the river.

Getting There

Proceed from Powers on FS 33 and in 9 miles turn right (W) at China Flat on FS 3353. The road crosses a bridge over the Coquille River's south fork and turns to gravel. You'll see signs for Mt. Barklow Trail, 11 miles. Refer to previous sections for notes about this route and use caution along narrow areas.

Lower trailhead: From China Flat, proceed on 3353 about 3.3 miles and turn left (S) on FS 5591 and follow it about 1.5 miles to a bridge across Johnson Creek. Across the bridge on the right side is the trailhead, with a primitive campsite. Once on foot from the campsite, follow the trail upriver along Sucker Creek about 0.2 mile and look for the trail on the other side of the river. Use caution when crossing the creek and do not attempt during high water.

Upper Trailhead: From China Flat, proceed on 3353. Refer to previous sections and use caution in narrow sections of road. In 11 miles is the parking area for Barklow Mountain Trail. Continue on 3353 and in about 2.5 miles turn left (E) on FS 260. This is going to be a rough, washboardy 1.5 miles down to the trailhead. The trail beings east of the parking area, through a dense stand of rhodies. It heads downhill through the canyon, on a course high above the creek. The trail traverses a steep section of fine, loose rock at one point, so take it easy!

Yontz Camp is about 0.5 mile down the canyon, in a small flat along a spring-fed sidestream that flows down to Sucker Creek. The trail proceeds down the canyon and encounters the Sucker Creek crossing. Use caution when crossing the creek and do not attempt during high water. Once across, follow a faint track about 0.2 mile downriver to a primitive campsite and the trailhead near FS 5591.

6. Iron Mountain Trail: Of the many Powers-region hikes, this is among the most remote and least strenuous. It's always rewarding. The 2.7-mile trail follows a ridgeline through part of Iron Mountain Botanical Area, a remarkably diverse bit of the Siskiyou National Forest that boasts more than 200 species of plants.

You can access trailheads at either end from gravel roads that offer spectacular views in themselves. Since the trail's relatively short and not too challenging, consider an out-and-back from one end or the other. The southern trailhead's easier to get to.

Getting There

Southern trailhead: From Powers, follow what eventually becomes FS 33 about 22 miles to Agness Divide and turn right (W) on FS 5325. Up we go! The road definitely roughens, but how about that view? Just drive slowly and enjoy! You'll pass side roads. About 6 miles from the divide is a "Y" intersection with FS 3340.

Bear right, staying on FS 5325. The route swings under a damp hillside of darlingtonia, a bug-eating type of pitcher plant. Up around a few bends, just under 6.5 miles from Agness Divide, is the trailhead for FS 1265.

Even the parking area has some interesting plants, hedged by low-lying greenery sometimes called squaw carpet that blooms with purple flowers in spring and early summer.

The trail heads up a former jeep road, passing a mix of Coast Range shrubbery ranging from azaleas to salal to rhodies, and dominated by manzanita. All four manzanita species found on the Powers Ranger District are represented here in the Iron Mountain Range, but what's really remarkable are all the other plants and wildflowers. The Powers Ranger District can provide you with some informative literature, and you'll have fun identifying purple flox, for example, but can you find piper's bluegrass? How about prince's pine (not a tree but a forb; *Chirnaphila umbellata*), grouseflowers (*Synthyris reniformis*), heart-leaved twayblades (*Listera cordata*) or nodding arnicas (*arnica cordifolia*)?

You'll also enjoy the mix of trees that include Port Orford cedar, white fir and several kinds of pines, from lodgepole to western white to sugar to knobcone to Jeffery.

The way levels off, with a side trail to the right (NE) to Iron Mountain Vista. Even on these steep cliffs, rhodies thrive, blooming in early June. Views really open up as you climb, and a clear day brings an ocean vista.

As noted, there once was a lookout here, but only bits of broken glass remain. Easier to spot are the succulents known as stonecrop that grow (and sometimes bloom) among the rocks. The rocks themselves support thriving colonies of lichen with such whimsical names as freckle pelt and frog lichen.

Spread over about 12 acres on the east and northern slopes of the summit are several hundred Brewer Spruce. Also known as weeping spruce because of their long, drooping branches, these trees are found only in the Siskiyou Mountains of northern California and southern Oregon, and this is the northernmost stand.

Back on the main trail, the route continues northward, passing a couple of other high points, and comes to an array of solar-powered radio antennas near the northern trailhead.

Northern trailhead: From Powers, follow signs to China Flat, Ilahee, Agness. The road becomes FS 33 about 4 miles from town. About 17.5 miles and turn right (W) on FS 3347, following signs to USFS Rock Creek campground. Continue past the campground, cross a bridge over Rock Creek and bear right on FS 3347. Follow the road about 12 miles to its terminus. The trail follows an old jeep road past radio antennas, then goes along a ridgeline past three prominent high points, the southernmost of which was once the site of a forest fire lookout tower.

22. Over Barklow Mountain: China Flat to Elk River

Road Conditions: *Gravel. Closed by snow in winter.*
Notes: *Route described is 50 miles; gravel for 40. About 150-mile roundtrip from Coos Bay.*

Not far from Powers along FS 33 (Coquille-Rogue Scenic Byway) is a challenging route to the coast, a gravel Forest Service road through the soaring Iron Mountain Range into the watershed of fabled Elk River.

The trip's high point is near 3,579-ft. Mt. Barklow, amidst still-uncut timber and panoramic ridgelines. From there, the route skirts down and down-canyon, delving in and around clefts of the imposing Iron Range massif, crossing feeder streams and oozing waterfalls, finally meeting Elk River, that emerald jewel.

Getting There
Proceed to Powers as described in chapter 18.

From Powers, stay on the main route, following signs to China Flat, Ilahe and Agness. The route becomes FS 33 about 4 miles from town. See chapter 18 for info about Elk Creek Falls and other sights.

About 12 miles out of Powers on FS 33 is China Flat, an unimproved campground courtesy of Georgia-Pacific, with limited facilities.

At China Flat, turn right (W) on FS 3353, following a sign to Butler Bar campground. Make a note of your mileage or zero out your trip odometer here.

The road crosses the river and heads into the woods, passing a sign indicating this way to US 101, 50 miles. Don't be scared, it's only going to take all day . . .

The road ascends gently through sunny southern slopes, the forest a rich mix of fir, cedar, big-leaf maple, red alder and western hemlock. The hardy madrone tree is another favorite, with that sensual, peeling bark revealing a bright red trunk beneath.

Wild rhododendrons put on their show of pink flowers in early June, and the rest of the summer brings a progression of wildflower blooms, dominated by distinctive spindles of purple foxglove.

Just over 3 miles from China Flat is a "Y" intersection with FS 5591. Bear right staying on FS 3353.

Your view west opens up, giving an indication of what lies ahead. And yes, those rugged hills will eventually have to be gotten over . . .

About 6 miles along is Boulder Creek, sometimes marked by a sign, deep in ferny shadows. A bit beyond is a rocky spire cropping up in the plunging canyons to the south. Also in this vicinity -- right along the road -- are the "Two Friends" trees pictured in this chapter. While not unusual for trees to topple against each other, it's remarkable that both trees continue to grow.

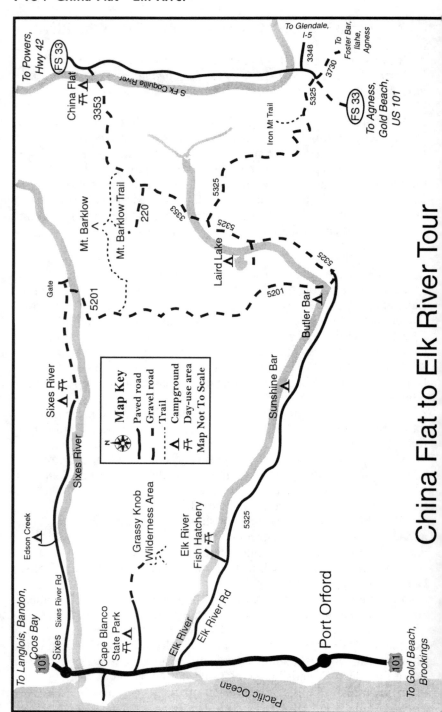

China Flat to Elk River Tour

"Two Friends" trees along Barklow Mountain Road

The route heads downhill through thick woods, passing a "T" intersection with FS 3363 on the right (N). Keep going on FS 3353, following signs to Butler Bar and US 101.

Not far along is a three-way "Y"; take the left fork. (The other two roads are marked FS 150 and 140).

The road heads down into a side canyon, crossing a little bridge and making a big "U" as it heads back out of the draw.

This next section requires alert driving, with some plunging drop-offs from the steep mountainside road. Take it slowly!

The road begins to crest the ridgeline, and at about 11 miles you'll encounter Mt. Barklow Trail. (See chapter 21.)

The Barklows were a pioneer family in the region whose ranks included early-day gold seekers and a colorful stagecoach driver, and in addition to a prominent peak carrying their name, this route is often called Barklow Mountain Road.

Continuing on the main route, bear left at the fork with FS 220, staying on FS 3353. The route descends, heading south below steep ridges. We've crossed the watershed divide, with feeder streams rushing toward the Elk River.

There's another "T" intersection at 12.5 miles. Bear right.

In less than 0.5 mile is yet another fork, a three-way this time. Take the route to the right, maintaining a southward direction on FS 3353.

The road stays at elevation, with views westward. The descent is subtle, with several stream crossings, including a lovely one at mile 15.5.

The route continues south, plying the sinews of Iron Mountain range. Ghostly white skeletons of cedar trees, victims of a devastating fire in the mid-1800s, stand by the hundreds on the mountainsides.

The road trends westward, crossing more sidestreams. At 20 miles you'll come to what feels like a major crossroad after all this isolation.

This is the end of FS 3353. Continue ahead (W), on FS 5325, with signs indicating US 101, 29 miles.

2 miles beyond is yet another "T", this one with FS 5502. Continue ahead (W) on FS 5325, following a sign to US 101, 27 miles.

Down and down we go! The route passes USFS Laird Lake campground at mile 23.5. The lake's a tiny gem in a primeval glen, its water possessed of the same clear, green intensity as the river it eventually feeds.

Following the main route, the road passes a fenceline and heads down a hillside rich with waterfalls and streams. Down and then some more, and at last here's the bottom, and Elk River.

To the right is FS 5201 to Sixes River. (See chapter 22.)

Here, too, is USFS Butler Bar campground, spread under a grove of big myrtles along a gravelly stretch of river. Pavement begins; it's about 18 miles downriver to US 101.

And what a ride! Steep canyon walls of huge trees soar up on either side, while the river bubbles over gravelly riffles and plunges through chasms. Tiny waterfalls seep down from the hillsides as the road hugs a little slice of land above the river. Clear, cold water looks green as it flows across the serpentine rock, and there are many spots to stop and test the waters with a swim. There are also USFS campgrounds and a handful of undeveloped camping sites along the way

A few scattered homes signal the return to civilization, and you'll also pass the state's Elk River Hatchery, where you can stop for a look or a picnic. Once at US 101, a left turn takes you to Port Orford (2 miles); turn right to return to Coos Bay (50 miles.)

22. Emerald Pathways: A Tour of Sixes and Elk Rivers

Road conditions: *Paved and gravel, with rough, steep and narrow sections. Subject to snow closure.*
Notes: *Route described, 55 miles; roundtrip total from Coos Bay, 155 miles.*

Among the treasures of the southern Oregon coast are a couple of small, pristine rivers that run from the uttermost reaches of the Coast Range, wild and clear to the sea.

Elk River and Sixes River, situated just north of Port Orford, are peaceful oases protected from summer winds and overlooked by most travelers. There are paved roads for many miles up both of them, along with picnic spots, fishing access, swimming holes, campgrounds, a fish hatchery and a stretch of river open to recreational gold seeking. You could spend days checking out either of them, but for some real fun take this trek across the watershed divide on a classic back road that traverses some of the most spectacular scenery in the region.

The Sixes River, once a source of gold-mining frenzy, is a classic meander through a wide coastal plain into deeply forested canyons.

The Elk is an emerald river of pure enchantment. It runs through narrow chasms of rock and pristine forest, with shallow gravel bars for wading and deep pools for inspiring swims. These grottos, so intensely green, are framed against soaring canyons of hanging fern gardens and ancient trees tilted at precarious angles over the narrow gorge.

Both are popular fishing rivers for those seeking salmon, steelhead and sea-run trout, depending on the time of year and a variety of other conditions, principally whether the rivers have silted in at their respective seaward confluences.

If you choose to make the loop, you'll be in for a bit of rough, gravel-road travel, and the road hugs some pretty meaningful twists and turns, but your reward is a limitless panorama of what is Oregon. You'll travel through grand old forest and sail along perhaps the most spectacular ridgeline route described in this book, before dropping down to that jewel, the Elk River.

Getting There

From Coos Bay, head south on US 101, passing Bandon in 25 miles and continuing south into Curry County along coastal benchlands that support cranberry bogs and pastureland.

Next is Langlois, sleepy settlement with a few stores and shops. The highway dips and rolls southward, passing tiny Denmark. A bit beyond, US 101 drops into a wide coastal plain around Sixes River. There's a last-chance grocery store. Turn left (E) on Sixes River Rd., following signs to BLM Edson Creek and Sixes River campgrounds. Another sign

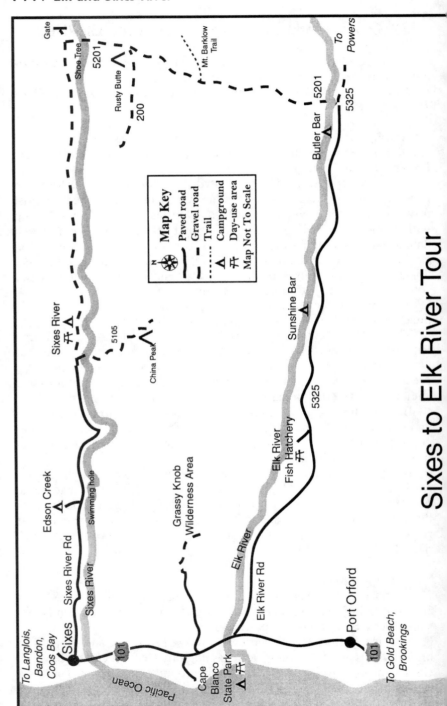

Sixes to Elk River Tour

indicates the operating status of the campgrounds. Note your odometer reading or zero out your trip odometer here.

The route rolls by a B&B and heads upriver, passing farms and a few residences, overlooking the river's progress through gravel bars and wide pools. Much of the riverfront is private property — fenced off in places – but there are a few places for informal public access.

The Sixes River drew plenty of attention in pioneer days once word got out about gold deposits, and piles of dredged rocks testify to mining operations. Small claims are still active, and well marked to keep people out. Today's miner wades into the river in wetsuit, goggles and snorkel, and uses a gasoline-powered suction pump mounted on inner tubes or pontoons to dredge through gravel and rocks for the precious ore.

Dozens of picturesque sidestreams and little waterfalls feed the river as the forest thickens and the canyon narrows.

This was once the land of the Tututne Indian, specifically a tribe known as Kwatami, who called the river "Sekewe'tce," meaning "wide open." It's not known whether this referred to the condition of the river at its mouth, or its meander through a wide coastal plain, or some other aspect.

Also unclear is the origin of "Sixes." It may have been the white man's pronunciation of the native name for the river. Some speculate that the name derives from a Chinook Indian term for "friend," which is pronounced "sixes." Others note the river's about six miles north of Port Orford.

At any rate, the "wide open" nature of the canyon narrows as you head upriver. At 4.3 miles is Edson Creek. The popular swimming hole here is called Cannonball. BLM Edson Creek campground is to the left.

A couple miles past that the road climbs away from the river, then becomes a single lane and passes a few homesteads. The trees get bigger, and the surroundings are taking on a park-like appearance.

Across a concrete bridge the road turns to gravel. Soon you'll encounter BLM Sixes River campground with a mile-long stretch of river open to gold panning and dredging. It's extremely popular, especially in summer, and truth be told, the gold's pretty much played out. But "everyone has fun." A display offers more information and there's usually a helpful camp host.

The site is open May through September for day-use and camping, with fees for both.

Continuing beyond the campground, pass private mining claims and a few side tracks as you climb through alders and ferns, with big firs soaring overhead.

At about 14 miles is a "Y" intersection; bear right and continue ahead, soon crossing a bridge over Big Creek. A sign says you're leaving the national forest. At about 16 miles you'll come to a "T" intersection, with the way straight ahead usually gated closed.

Unique road marker at FS 5201

Turn right (S), on FS 5201 The junction is marked by a tree festooned with dozens of shoes and boots. I've never gotten the same explanation twice about how all this started, but it's a great landmark.

Say goodbye to the Sixes River; the route crosses a concrete bridge and begins some serious climbing up a wide, well-graded road. You'll get some glimpses of the view to the east on the way up, and perhaps notice some milepost markers. This route was badly damaged -- as were many others in the region -- during a ferocious storm in 1996, and it took the Forest Service a couple of years to reopen it. You'll notice extensive rockwork in some of the ravines and canyons to replace land that had washed out.

The byway crests at about the 21-mile mark, at a "T" intersection with FS 200 to the right (W). Continue straight on the main road.

There's nothing like being up on these high ridges to get a true perspective of how many thousands of acres lie between the coast and the outside world. Not so much as the glint off a fire lookout tower is revealed, and save for the occasional patch of clearcut, it's an unbroken sea of timber as far as the eye can see.

Many areas have been logged through the years, of course, but vigorous regrowth is under way Just contemplating how these rugged canyons were logged in the first place will give you renewed respect for the back-breaking work that goes into timber cutting.

The road continues southward, rolling at elevation and offering views west. There's a bit of everything along here -- trees new and old, dry rocky slopes, tiny waterfalls in ferny ravines.

Just under 24 miles, bear left as the route passes a pair of roads heading west. About a mile past that is a parking area for FS Trail 1258 to Mt. Barklow.

(**Trail notes:** This is a rugged push up to the 3,579-ft. peak, once site of a lookout tower. There's a collapsed shack on a lower slope, but the tower was removed by helicopter. The trail continues, intersecting with Barklow Mt. Rd. (See chapter 23.)

Not far from the trail marker, it's time for the show. Here are those commanding views I promised: east and south open on a seemingly-endless sea of trees, while westward forests are halted only by the Pacific Ocean. The road descends a bit and encounters a brief paved section along a sheer rock wall. On a ridgeline now, we're straddling the watershed divide of the Sixes and Elk Rivers.

At a "Y" intersection with FS 350, bear right, following the main road, FS 5201. A couple miles past that, at a "T" intersection with FS 390, bear left, staying on FS 5201. The road takes a more abrupt descent, and you'll still be seeing milepost markers from time to time.

If you visit in early summer, rocky hillsides along here will be blanketed with tiny wildflowers, while other hardy plants such as Oregon grape cling to precarious perches. Wild rhododendrons pop out everywhere, even along the highest ridgeline, almost as if they'd been set here and there to add to this spectacular drive. What a treat to be here when they bloom in early June!

The road skirts along plunging canyons, switchbacking down toward Elk River, and suddenly here it is, at about 33 miles into your trip. Just across a bridge is USFS Butler Bar campground, in a stand of huge myrtlewoods and firs.

Here also is pavement again, and signs indicating the end of FS 5201 and the beginning of FS 5325. Head right (W), following signs to US 101, 19 miles. (For details on FS 5325 to Powers, see chapter 22.)

The route downriver must have fallen out of heaven. Magnificent trees jut at dramatic angles along the canyon, while the river plunges through gravel bars, deep pools and whitewater cataracts. The steep slopes of the canyon walls are thick with gigantic swordferns and luxuriant undergrowth, while dozens of tiny trickles and larger tributaries course down through elfin nooks and crannies to the main river.

There are USFS campgrounds at Butler Bar, Panther Creek and Sunshine Bar, and dozens of turnouts, picnic spots and unofficial camping

Deep, clear pools beckon along the Elk River

places offering opportunities to take in the beauty of Elk River.

Some stretches have easy access for wading, while other sections require some scrambling to get to the deep gorges and those fabled emerald grottos.

Part of the pristine condition of Elk River canyon is guaranteed by the existence of the Grassy Knob Wilderness Area, which officially begins on the north side of the river and takes in a few square miles from there. (There's no access from the river; for details, see chapter 24.)

What the Indians called Elk River is not quite the object of spirited discussion as is the Indian name for Sixes River. Port Orford writer Pat Masterson, a descendent of early settlers, said the Indian name for Elk River was *Ti-tu-na*, which sounds a lot like the name of the tribe, *Titune*. What it meant isn't known.

As the river canyon begins to widen a bit, homesteads appear. Next landmark is the state fish hatchery, getting salmon and steelhead ready for release into the Elk and Chetco Rivers. There's an interpretive display, and you're welcome to wander around the holding pools.

The route meanders along the widening river plain, past more homes and ranches and a large RV park, back to US 101. Port Orford is 2 miles south (left); Coos Bay is 50 miles north.

24. Port Orford's Back Door

Road conditions: *Paved and gravel.*
Notes: *Three day-hikes in the Port Orford area.*

Port Orford is one of the most picturesque places on the southern Oregon coast, and among the first places for white explorers to settle. Yet it remains a classic small coastal town -- population about 1000-- while offering some outstanding nearby recreational opportunities often overlooked by visitors hurrying through on US 101. It also boasts one of the most unusual fishing docks on the coast.

While the Port Orford headlands create a sheltered harbor for boats, the headlands aren't enough to fend off the full onslaught of the sea, so fishing vessels are hoisted out of the water and "moored" on trailers on the dock. You can drive right down onto the dock, check out the action, and often buy fresh fish.

Port Orford has a handful of restaurants, motels, galleries, and souvenir and collectibles shops, and a lovely beach at the foot of historic Battle Rock. Vehicles are allowed to drive on the beach.

Up on the headlands are a couple of short walks that give you some stunning overviews of the area, and not far from town are two longer hikes with splendid views. In addition, Cape Blanco State Park is just north of Port Orford, offering tours of a historic lighthouse and restored pioneer ranch, as well as camping, hiking and equestrian trails and intriguing beachwalks.

Port Orford Heads State Park: Panoramic headlands and a former Coast Guard station are now part of a day-use area that includes hiking paths and interpretive center. The interpretive center is open for tours April 1 – Oct 31, 10 a.m. to 3:30 p.m.; closed Tuesdays and Wednesdays.)

Getting There: From U.S. 101 in Port Orford, watch for state park signs at 9th St., near the big curve in the middle of town. Follow the road about 1 mile up the hill to the park.

Built during the 1920s and '30s, the Coast Guard station was one of the three earliest in Oregon, and retains much of its original architecture. Of equal interest is an adjacent building that serves as the park manager's residence. Also intact are period outbuildings, garages and plantings. The lawns are kept neatly trimmed by wild but nonchalant deer which can often be spotted browsing along the margins of the park. And overhead the grand old Sitka spruce preside.

From here, crews went down a path to a 504-step stairway to a boathouse, which burned in the 1970s. Another path led to a lookout tower. The existing walkways have been expanded into three short trails around the headlands, all of which begin south of the interpretive center.

The Lookout Trail is a charmer, a narrow ribbon of old concrete lined

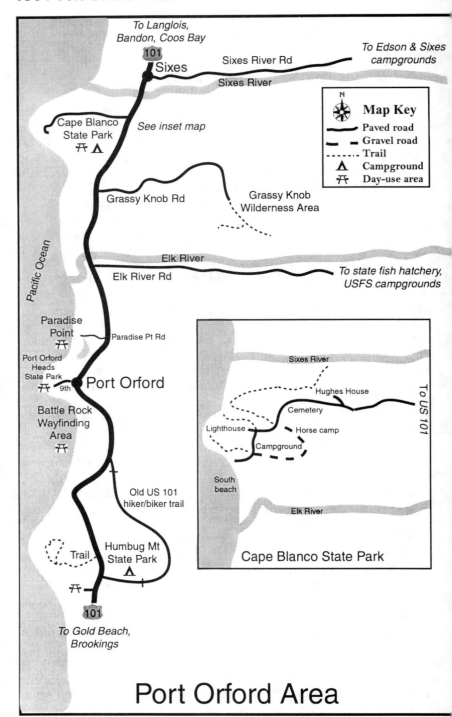

To Langlois,
Bandon, Coos Bay

101 Sixes

Sixes River Rd

To Edson & Sixes
campgrounds

Sixes River

Map Key

N

— Paved road
– – Gravel road
⋯ Trail
Δ Campground
⊼ Day-use area

Cape Blanco
State Park
⊼ Δ

See inset map

Grassy Knob Rd

Grassy Knob
Wilderness Area

Pacific Ocean

Elk River

Elk River Rd

To state fish hatchery,
USFS campgrounds

Paradise
Point
⊼

Paradise Pt Rd

Port Orford
Heads
State Park
⊼ 9th

Port Orford

Battle Rock
Wayfinding
Area
⊼

Old US 101
hiker/biker trail

Trail

Humbug Mt
State Park
Δ

⊼

101

To Gold Beach,
Brookings

Cape Blanco State Park inset:

Sixes River

Hughes House

Cemetery

Lighthouse

Horse camp

Campground

South
beach

Elk River

To US 101

Cape Blanco State Park

Port Orford Area

Lookout Trail at Port Orford Heads State Park

with iris plants that bloom purple through much of the summer. Sheltered by wind-sculpted trees, it leads to the site of a former lookout. Brush has grown up around the fenced vista area, but the view is still nice.

You can loop back on Headlands Trail, which roams out along the western flanks, with heart-stopping ocean views and side paths leading to further overlooks. Another loop option takes you from the Lookout Trail onto a path that offers a look down at the site of the former boathouse, along with some fantastic southward views. There are benches on which you can perch and study all manner of things: the curving-away coastline and steeply rising Curry County hills, seabirds swirling on tricky air currents, fishing boats motoring slowly homeward, perhaps a whale's plume out in the rolling sea. You loop back to the parking area from this trail as well.

Grassy Knob Wilderness Area

Grassy Knob must be the definitive wilderness area, since this 15,000-acre pocket of old-growth forest between the Sixes and Elk rivers doesn't even have an official hiking trail through it.

Grassy Knob was among a number of small wilderness set-asides created in the 1980s to save stands of unlogged forest and protect valued watersheds. Grassy Knob does both, preserving some awesome trees while buffering the nationally-designated wild and scenic Elk River.

Still, it lacks the offerings of other wilderness areas: rivers, lakes, geologic features, historical sites, and, as mentioned, developed trails. Some intrepid types notice it on a map and try to explore, only to be confronted with walls of rugged, plunging canyons, with few flat areas even to pitch a tent.

You can, however, drive part way into Grassy Knob Wilderness Area, and take a short hike to 2342-ft. Grassy Knob, which offers spectacular views of the surrounding forest and nearby sea.

Getting There

From Port Orford, head north on US 101 for 4 miles and turn right (E) on Curry County 196, Grassy Knob Rd.

(From Coos Bay, head south on US 101 about 46 miles. About 0.25 mile beyond the Cape Blanco State Park turn, take a left (E) on Curry County 196, Grassy Knob Rd.)

Pavement heads uphill, passing cranberry bogs, pastures and a couple of residences. The county lane ends at 4.2 miles, as does pavement. Continue, and in 0.1 of mile you'll encounter a "Y" intersection; take the right fork, Forest Service 5105.

You'll get glimpses of the ocean as the route climbs through mixed-species forest. The road tops out, roller-coasters down, then up again.

Off to either side is officially wilderness, steep canyons of it. The lane ends about 8 miles up, where a USFS sign, if intact, has a brief description of the trail to Grassy Knob, 1.4 miles.

The trail is a continuation of the road, bermed and trenched to keep out vehicles. A profusion of young fir trees sprout in the trail.

Head up through the woods, enjoying wildflowers and wild rhodies. After about 10 minutes, watch for rocks on the ground that form an arrow pointing right (W) to Grassy Knob. The footpath goes up meadow-like slopes, cuts into a stand of trees and comes to a rock stairway, remnant of the fire-lookout days. Atop the stairs, you're standing where the tower was, with views south and west. Wow!

You can look down to the harbor at Port Orford, and get glimpses of Elk River meandering in canyons to the south.

The watchtower that once stood here had a brush with infamy in World War II, when spotters saw a Japanese plane buzz the forest and let loose a bomb. The bomb, which didn't go off and still hasn't been found, was one of hundreds of incendiary devices dropped on or ballooned into Pacific Northwest forests to start fires. The Japanese hoped to create panic and force the diversion of manpower to fire fighting.

Return on the footpath to the main trail, then back down the way you came, to the parking area.

(In case you're curious, the logging track continues southeast past the lookout path for 0.75 mile and ends abruptly. It was built just before wilderness status was granted in the mid-1980s, and never used.)

Retrace your footsteps, then your auto route, for a return to US 101 and turn left (S) to continue to Port Orford; Coos Bay is 50 miles north.

Humbug Mountain

Although the scope of this book officially ends at Port Orford, it's not fair to leave out such a popular destination so close to town. There's a campground and day-use area, as well as a 3-mile trail to the top that offers some terrific views. Also near the campground is an old portion of Coast Highway turned into a hiker/biker trail.

As for the name, again we have some debate. It was originally called Sugar Loaf Peak, and anyone gazing upon it could understand why. In his *Guide to Oregon South Coast History*, author Nathan Douthit says that Port Orford founder William Tichenor sent a party of men to "find a good route to the interior. He told the men to head south . . . Instead the party got lost, wandered as far north as the Coquille River, and when it returned took out its frustration by changing the name Sugar Loaf Peak to Tichenor's Humbug."

Another version has the party struggling to the mountaintop to get their bearings, only to find they were less than a dozen miles from town.

It's upon these things and others you may ponder as you wander up Humbug's flanks on trails that lead through inspiring stands of old-growth fir, spruce and Port Orford cedar.

Getting There

From Port Orford, head south on US 101 for 4 miles to Humbug Mountain State Park. The trailhead parking area is the first thing you'll see, on the right, immediately adjacent to US 101. The camping area (and hiker/biker trail) is just beyond on the left. You can also drive through the campground to the west end to access the beach. The day-use area is a bit beyond, on the right side of US 101.

Trail notes: The trail begins in a grove of huge, mossy myrtlewood trees, with grizzled old Port Orford cedars towering on the steep slopes above. Storms in recent years have brought down branches and some large trees, and the distinctive smells of these two aromatic species mingle along the creek and canyon. Breathe deeply! You'll need it, because the first half-mile of this trail is the toughest.

Mileposts every half-mile tell your progress, so you'll know when you've conquered the first big challenge. After that, the trail's well-engineered switchbacks make the rest of the climb not so daunting. The trail rises higher and higher above US 101. Just under 1 mile is a crossroads, where a sign informs the West Trail is 1.5 miles to the summit, and East Trail 2 miles. The East Trail is less strenuous, so we'll go that way. The trail makes its way around to the east side of the mountain, where clumps of basket grass and huckleberry appear. The conifer forest gives way to drier slopes of spindly tanoaks. The trail swings back around to the west slopes and meets the West Trail for the final push.

The forested top of Humbug doesn't afford much of a view, but there's a bench with a fine vista south, clear down to Frankport Rocks and Nesika Beach. On the way down, return on the West Trail and you'll be rewarded with the best views of the hike. Here, too, are benches, and the views this time look north to Port Orford and Cape Blanco, its lighthouse blinking at intervals. Continue down the trail to the junction of the East and West Trails, and from there back to the parking area.

Cape Blanco State Park: See chapter 5.

PART THREE
The Umpqua and Smith Rivers

Largest river between San Francisco Bay and the Columbia River, the Umpqua River finds its source high in the Cascade Range, meandering many miles to its outlet near Reedsport and Winchester Bay. From Reedsport, busy Highway 38 runs along the Umpqua for part of its journey to inland valleys and Interstate 5. The Umpqua is prized for fishing opportunities, and there are a handful of other recreational opportunities along its shores. In the Reedsport vicinity are the Dean Creek Elk Viewing Area, Brandy Bar State Park, and the access road to Loon Lake. (See chapters 10, 11 & 12 for details.)

The Smith River is a tributary that enters the mighty Umpqua not far from Reedsport, and it serves as a portal to a forest wonderland that sees few visitors. Miles of paved and gravel back-country roads roam the river canyons and ridgelines, passing waterfalls, swimming holes, hiking trails, campgrounds and soaring mountaintops. Best of all, you can take in many of the best sights on loop tours lasting from a few hours to a couple of days.

Smith River Road is also a potential back way to Eugene, and doesn't actually take much longer than better-known routes. Unless, I hope, you're inspired to stop for a picnic at a waterfall!

Wildlife abounds in the Smith River region, especially up the river's north fork. Birds range from colorful woodpeckers to coolly soaring hawks to distinctive, white-maned bald eagles, while down on the ground you might spot chipmunks, squirrels, skunks and raccoons. After dusk, bats! And don't be surprised to come upon slightly larger furry mammals: some healthy looking bears live up here, and there are bobcats and cougars, too.

Four tours are presented in this section, the second of which, the entire Smith River Highway, is a lot of driving to and from Coos Bay for a single day, so consider an overnight expedition. The other three are easy day-trips.

Start all tours by heading north from Reedsport on US 101. Cross the Umpqua River Bridge and turn right (E) on Smith River Rd.

It never ceases to amaze me how traffic almost instantly evaporates once you get on our less-traveled roads, and this route not far from busy US 101 is a prime example. Still, all it takes is one maniac who won't move over to share a narrow byway and you've got the equivalent of any bad freeway crash, **so take it easy and stay alert!**

25. Smith River to Vincent Creek

Road conditions: *110-mile loop from Coos Bay. Paved, year-round access.*
Notes: *Camping, fishing, swimming. Wildflowers line the back roads in spring and summer; fall colors are terrific.*

This is a sweet little look at the Smith River region, with a jaunt back over the watershed divide between the Smith and Umpqua rivers. You return via Highway 38 to Reedsport. The next chapter continues the rest of the Smith River route from Vincent Creek to Highway 38 near Drain and Interstate 5.

Getting There
From Reedsport, follow US 101 north, crossing the Umpqua River Bridge, and turn right (E) on Smith River Rd. The road crosses a trestle and heads up the river's north bank.

The water runs wide and mighty along here, a mix of freshwater flow and tidal influence, just part of the far-flung estuary that commingles the Umpqua and Smith rivers.

The farmlands are lush, some with as many as three barns full of hay. The hillsides show signs of logging, but the lower slopes and the river canyon are picturesque, with roadside trees green and glowing spring and summer, ablaze with color in fall.

Just over 3 miles, you'll cross Hudson Slough. About 3.5 miles up is Stowe Marsh, one of the only places along the Smith River left in its natural state. To see this wildlife preserve, turn right (S) on Southside Rd., crossing a bridge over Smith River. Look for signs on the right just across the bridge. Marsh wren, green heron and a variety of waterfowl are among the birds in residence in this reedy wetland.

Continuing on Smith River Rd., you'll pass a few homesteads and old ranches, but the country is becoming less populated with every mile. About 8 miles upriver is USFS Noel Ranch picnic area, and about 3 miles beyond that, Riverside County Park, where there's a boat ramp and picnic tables. A couple miles past that is a BLM sign declaring this Smith River Timber Access Road, and providing some mileages. You'll notice a slight difference in pavement, and the absence of roadway lines and stripes.

Tidewater ends about 20 miles up, and in summer the river shrinks to the depth of your ankle in most places, with deeper pools here and there.

This is a diverse forest, full of old fir, hemlock and Sitka spruce. The road runs through classic overarching canopies of alder, its white bark reminiscent of birch. Exposed rock walls along the lane sometimes take on the appearance of a brooding face, sort of like those monoliths on Easter Island.

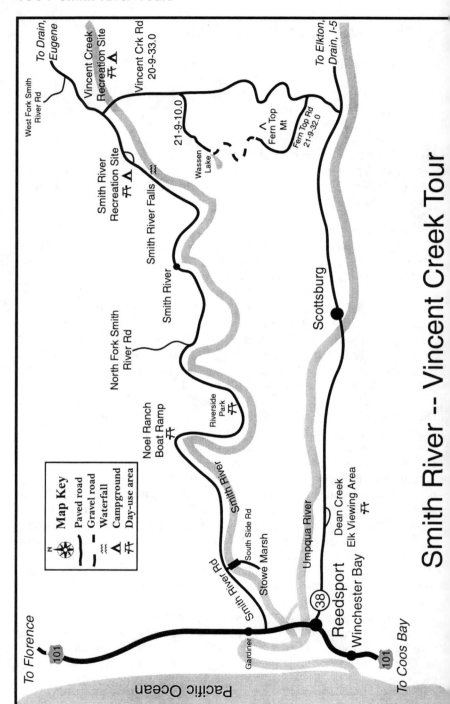

Smith River -- Vincent Creek Tour

Cows cross right on schedule on Smith River Road

There are dozens of places to stop and picnic or camp along the way, and even if you're not doing either, I always advocate taking a break to soak in the scenery. As nice as the drive is, you'll always notice more things when you stop!

Smith River Falls is about 25 miles upriver. The falls are modest as these things go, set amidst rocks carved through with channels and pools. The pools make great swimming holes. A tunnel takes fish around the falls in low water times. Fingerlings mill around in the pools near the tunnel entry and exit, and sometimes a big one darts out of a deep hole.

Just up around the bend from the falls is BLM Smith River recreation site, with day-use area and campground.

The road continues upriver, and about 30 miles along is BLM Vincent Creek recreation site, with day-use area and campground set amidst nice green lawns under spreading broadleaf and evergreen trees.

Smith River Rd. continues for many miles upriver, but for this tour, we'll turn here at Vincent Creek. (See the following chapter for the continued tour up Smith River.)

Turn right (S) on Vincent Creek Rd., following signs to Wells Creek and Highway 38, 15 miles.

What a sweet little road! Paved all the way, surrounded by a true mixed-species forest, and fanned-over with a leafy ceiling of alders. Spring brings vibrant greenery and wildflowers, and the autumn colors are as good as it gets in coastal country. The creek itself is a little trickle in late summer and autumn, much more robust in raintime.

Get ready to traverse a watershed divide, which means we'll be climbing some mountains. In this case, we're traveling from the Smith River to the Umpqua River, and as is so often the case, the view from the top is spectacular.

The divide is marked by 1,856-ft Fern Top Mountain, around which the route skirts before dropping down to the Umpqua River.

There are some pretty good views from Vincent Creek Rd., but for the real thing you must go up Fern Top Rd. You'll see a sign directing you that way at an intersection not long after you've started to drop down toward the Umpqua. It's about 4 miles to Highway 38 from this intersection. Fern Top Rd. will take you back up the mountain for a mile or so, but the backtrack's worth it.

Check out the views north and south from the mountaintop road. As far as the eye can see, not a sign of civilization — save for clearcuts. Far below to the south you can spot sinews of the Umpqua River glistening in the sun.

And so quiet . . . just the sighing of huge trees, a shimmering rattle of alder leaves, occasional woodpecker knock and eagle's cry . . .

When you decide to quit your mountain realm, it's just a matter of a half-dozen miles to Wells Creek and Highway 38 along the Umpqua River. Turn right (west), following signs to Reedsport.

You'll soon encounter Scottsburg, founded at the height of gold fever in the Oregon Territory. This was as far up the Umpqua as ships from San Francisco and other ports could get. From here the trails went inland, to such gold boomtowns as Jacksonville.

Historic plaques explain details. Highway 38 crosses a bridge just beyond Scottsburg and continues downriver to Reedsport and US 101.

Along the way is the Dean Creek Elk Viewing Area, with a resident herd of Roosevelt elk that usually grazes in one of the protected pastures. An interpretive site offers more information, and you can also try your luck at spotting some of the other species of animals and birdlife that call this area home.

26. Smith River — Vincent Creek to Drain

Road conditions: *Paved, year-round access.*
Notes: *See previous chapter. Total loop from Coos Bay, 145 miles. Camping, fishing, boating.*

This continues the trip on Smith River Road begun last chapter. It describes the route from Vincent Creek to Drain, with a return on Highway 38 to Reedsport. Also included are details on continuing to Eugene.

Getting There

Refer to the previous chapter for directions to BLM Vincent Creek recreation site, 30 miles up Smith River Rd. from US 101. From Vincent Creek, continue east on Smith River Rd. You'll pass West Fork Smith River Rd. in about 2.5 miles. The road continues upriver through country

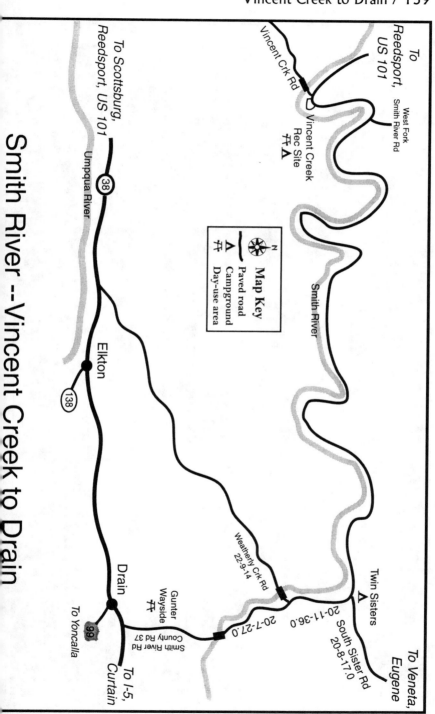

Smith River -- Vincent Creek to Drain

Smith River Falls glides over wide, flat rocks

that reflects the region's forest management techniques: clearcuts, regrowth areas, moderate-aged woods and a few stands of old, mixed-species trees. About 5 miles from Vincent Creek is the Carpenter Fir, a huge, 500-year-old Douglas fir that escaped the region's many forest fires, not to mention loggers!

On the subject of fire, a sign about 2 miles past Carpenter Fir describes the 1966 Oxbow Burn, which burned more than 43,000 acres. The area was replanted aerially -- a technique no longer used.

About 12 miles from Vincent Creek is a "T" intersection, not very well marked. An unimproved camping area, the Sisters Recreation site, is just north of the intersection. The road continues east to Eugene and other destinations. *(Eugene notes: It's about 45 miles from here to Eugene. Follow signs to Veneta, Territorial Highway and Eugene. You'll also have options along the way for routes to Cottage Grove and points south of Eugene.)*

To continue Smith River tour: Turn right (S) on Smith River Rd., BLM 20-11-36.0, following signs to Weatherly Creek and Highway 38. A sign if intact informs that Highway 38 is 21 miles. The way gets a bit rougher, following the river and passing secluded camping spots. Moss grows on shaded trees, and tiny waterfalls hide in shadowy grottos along the slopes. You'll cross a bridge about 4.5 miles from the Sisters intersection, with the river on the left for awhile, then another bridge puts the river back on the right.

8 miles from Sisters at a junction with Weatherly Creek Rd., bear left on what's now BLM 20-11-36.0. You'll pass more tucked-away encampments and travel through miles of remote country. In another mile is a "Y" intersection; bear left on what's now BLM 20-7-27.0, Smith River Rd.

On and on you go, past many roads and turnouts; in another 5 miles the pavement widens and sprouts center stripes and fog lines. Can "civilization" be far?

Some of the intimacy of the route may be lost, be we're still a long way from anywhere. The pioneer town of Gunter was situated near here, although not much remains. Powerlines appear, as do some homesteads. You'll pass South Fork Smith River Rd., BLM 21-5-18.0. The road angles into a north-south running valley.

In a few more miles is BLM Gunter Wayside, a day-use area in a former campground. In this vicinity we're traversing the watershed divide of the Smith and Umpqua rivers; the next few miles will bring sharp downhill sections as you drop toward Umpqua River and Highway 38.

A left (E) turn at Highway 38 will take you over to I-5 in a matter of moments, while a right turn heads into Drain, and from there, it's about 50 miles back to Reedsport.

27. Kentucky Falls and A Nose Named Roman

Road conditions: *Paved with gravel sections; subject to snow closure in extreme conditions.*
Notes: *120-mile loop from Coos Bay. Camping, fishing.*

This tour heads up Smith River's north fork, a trip that involves a dozen river crossings on the way to some wonderful waterfalls. After a hike to Kentucky Falls, we'll keep going for a look from atop mighty Roman Nose Mountain, then descend the west fork of Smith River and return along the main stem the way we came.

There are three short gravel stretches, but otherwise it's all paved roads, many of which travel along soaring ridgelines that offer commanding views in every direction.

Getting There
From Reedsport, head north on US 101 and turn right (E) on Smith River Road. Note your odometer reading or zero out your trip odometer here. The road crosses a causeway and returns to land on the river's north side.

You'll notice an instant change of pace on good old Smith River Road: No traffic!

The river, still under tidal influence, cuts a wide swath, and old footings and pilings attest to one-time commerce. The byway rambles through some sleepy countryside, at times passing through the middle of farms.

You'll pass USFS Noel Ranch picnic area in about 8 miles; Riverside County Park, with boat ramp and picnic tables, is about 11.5 miles. A couple miles beyond is a BLM sign declaring this the Smith River Timber Access Rd., and providing mileages. Roadway striping disappears.

About 15 miles up, turn left (N) on North Fork Rd., Douglas County 48A, also FS 48.

To the right, the river runs through fields choked with blackberry vines; the road hugs the steep canyon walls to the left. Wildflowers and tiny waterfalls flash by, and you get glimpses of mighty forests up on high ridges westward. Other slopes show signs of recent logging.

The river offers up some whitewater sections as it narrows up-canyon. At about 22 miles, you'll encounter a one-lane bridge and the first of nearly a dozen crossings of the north fork. The route turns to gravel on the other side, and passes a residence. Beyond a rough bit of gravel and replanted forest, just past a USFS boundary sign, the road becomes a delightful forest lane, bisecting a natural colonnade of alder trees that shelters huge swordferns, wildflowers and lush undergrowth, including the orange-fruited salmonberry. You might spot tiger lilies nodding in the breeze, and pass whole hillsides of wild iris.

Just under 24 miles is the second bridge crossing of the North Fork,

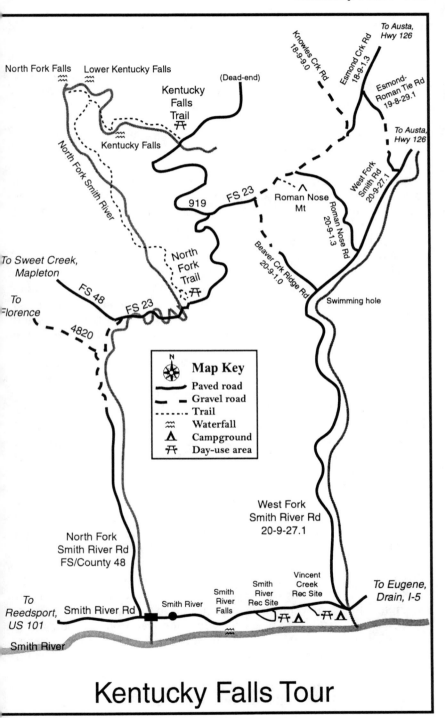

Kentucky Falls Tour

and at 24.9 miles you'll pass an intersection with roads to the left. Bear right (E), staying on North Fork Rd., FS 48, following a sign to Mapleton, 21 miles.

In less than a mile is another river crossing -- this one is the West Branch -- and a "T" intersection. Turn right (E) onto paved FS 23, following signs to Kentucky Falls Trail, 13; Roman Nose, 13, and two rock pits.

More beautiful forest . . . and don't I wish my driveway were this nicely paved and landscaped!

Cross the river yet again, then go over a cattle guard, passing a homestead. Another cattle guard, then more wondrous woodlands thick with salmonberry and other undergrowth. The late spring wildflower show can be fantastic, with wild rhodies in bloom and the white pom-pons of ocean spray listing in the breeze.

More river crossings . . . each intensely rewarding, each unique, but that's life, eh?

While all coastal rivers are characterized by what seems like a tortuously-convoluted route to the ocean, the Smith River's north fork may be the best example of the word "meandering." There actually was a river *Maender*, later called *Menderes*, famous for the many twists and turns it took in its 250-mile course to the Aegean sea. Also in the same region -- around what today is Turkey -- is another, shorter river flowing into the Dardenelles that was called, variously, Scamander, Menderes and Meander.

At about 29.5 miles is the parking area for North Fork Trail. This 8-mile trail passes through old-growth forest on its way to Kentucky Falls. **Trail notes**: *The first section of trail is level and well graveled. A few minutes of walking takes you across a wooden footbridge, and just beyond that, the trail forks; this is the beginning of a short loop, so you can go either way. The two trails link up again at a distinctive "twin fir" through which the trail continues as more modest footpath; or, you can return on the loop to the trailhead. The trail crosses two footbridges over the North Fork as it continues upriver. About 4 miles from the parking area is one of the trek's highlights, an old-growth fir 11 feet in diameter. The trail continues following the river and meets the trail to Lower Kentucky Falls.*

The road begins to climb uphill just past the parking area for North Fork Trail. At 35.3 miles you'll come to a "T" intersection. Turn left (W), remaining on pavement, following signs to Kentucky Falls, 3 miles.

Here also are woods thick with wild rhododendrons: rhodies left, rhodies right, rhodies growing out of solid rock right along the road. After some sweeping and climbing, the way reveals grand views south and west. There are a couple of interpretive signs along the way, and before long you'll reach Kentucky Falls "Special Interest Area."

An easy 0.75-mile trail takes you to Kentucky Falls. Keep going on the trail for another 1.75 miles to view the unique twin-waterfall enchantment of Lower Kentucky Falls and North Fork Smith River Falls. Just before the lower falls area is the "top end" of North Fork Trail.

Back at the trailhead, retrace your auto route back to the last major intersection with FS 23. To your right (S) is the way you came. Now go straight, onto gravel roadway, following signs (if in place) to Mapleton and Highway 126.

In less than 1 mile, you'll pass a "Leaving Siuslaw National Forest" sign and cross over onto clearcut BLM land. The road rolls over ridges, and in less than 1 mile encounters an unmarked "Y" intersection. Take the left (NE) fork.

Now you're flying along a ridgeline again, with views far to the north.

You're climbing the back side of Roman Nose Mountain, elevation 2,862 ft. Crest the hill at about 40 miles. To your right is a jeep trail you can park beside and walk up to the top of Roman Nose. (A gate keeps out traffic.)

The view goes all the way to the Pacific Ocean. There's a lookout tower and lots of microwave transmission dishes, complete with a noisy diesel generator.

Roman Nose is the highest of a couple of adjacent promontories, which may explain why early settlers called it Saddle Mountain. Lewis McArthur's *Oregon Geographic Names* says too many other peaks were called Saddle Mountain, so government surveyors suggested Roman Nose. Perhaps they felt it reflected some noble aspect of ancient

Neighboring cascades of Lower Kentucky and North Fork Falls

empire, for the mountaintop doesn't actually much resemble a nose. A nearby peak, lower in elevation and topped off with a huge rockslide on one side and an active quarry operation on the other, seems more nose-like, whether Roman or not, than the hilly plateau above it.

Back at the crest of the road, proceed over the top. To the right, at the foot of a rocky outcrop, is an old quarry pit, filled with green water. Just past that is a three-way "Y" intersection, with the middle fork (to on-going quarrying operations) gated off. Take the far left (NE) fork.

The way heads down through regrowth, seriously downhill and encounters another "Y" intersection. Go right, onto a paved road, following signs to Highway 126. This is Dunne Ridge Rd., BLM 19-8-29.1.

In less than 1 mile, at another "Y," go right again, following signs to Esmond Ck. Rd., still on paved BLM 19-8-29.1

At about mile 47 in this journey, you'll encounter a rough stretch of gravel road, but it lasts less than one mile.

At mile 50 is yet another "Y" intersection. Turn right (W). This will be West Fork Smith River Rd., BLM 27.1

Follow it, corkscrewing down from the ridgelines. You'll cross the west fork, pass a little frog pond on the right, along with several roads to the right with signs pointing to Kentucky Falls. Just stick to the main route, and at mile 63 encounter the intersection with Smith River Rd. Turn right (W) and follow the main stem of the river westward.

Just around the corner is BLM Vincent Creek recreation site, and a few miles down the road is BLM Smith River Falls recreation site, and the falls themselves.

Comport yourselves accordingly, given your recent experiences with waterfalls. That is to say, stop and have fun for awhile.

Whoo hoo!

Then continue downriver for a return to Reedsport.

28. Sweetest of Them All: Sweet Creek Falls

Road conditions: *Paved and gravel. Year-round access.*
Notes: *130-mile roundtrip from Coos Bay.*

I've saved the best for last. This fourth Smith River tour heads up the river's north fork through miles of forest to Sweet Creek, an enchanting USFS day-use area with waterfalls and pools linked by trails and catwalks above the river.

The drive continues, looping down to Woahink Lake, emerging at US 101 south of Florence. I've included an alternate route via Mapleton for a return down the Siuslaw River to Florence.

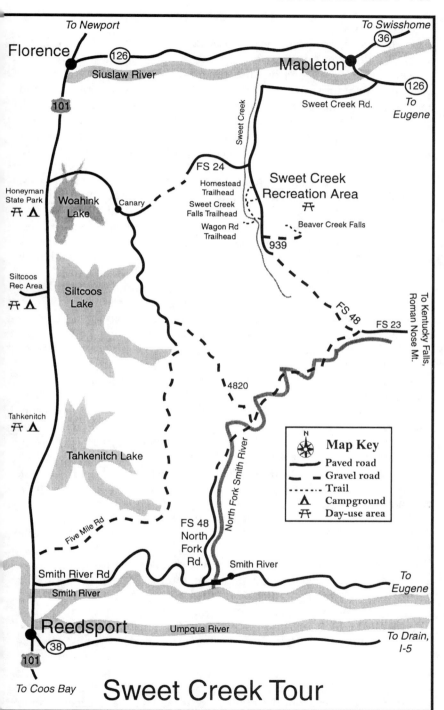

Sweet Creek Tour

Getting There

From Reedsport, head north on US 101 and turn right (E) on Smith River Rd. Note your mileage or zero out your trip odometer here.

Refer to chapter 25 for details of the trip upriver.

15 miles up, turn left (N) North Fork Rd., (Douglas County 48A and FS 48). The road heads up a narrow valley, passing pastures and cutbank places along the creek. Vast areas are swallowed by blackberry vines.

To the left are rocky embankments aglow with rockfast wildflowers, others oozing tiny waterfalls. Side canyons offer tantalizing views up to thicker forests.

The river begins a subtle change, running now through rocky riffles.

At about 22 miles, you'll encounter a one-lane bridge and the first of nearly a dozen crossings of the north fork. The route turns to gravel on the other side, and slips by a homestead. After passing through a recently-logged area, and going by a Siuslaw Forest Service boundary sign, the road rolls through storybook forest, shaded by alders and thick with ferns, wildflowers and salmonberry. What a charming lane!

At about 23 miles, cross another bridge and in 1 mile bear right (E) at a "Y" intersection, following FS 48, and a sign to Mapleton, 21.

In less than a mile is another river crossing -- this one the West Branch -- and a "T" intersection. Turn left (W), remaining on gravel FS 48. The byway is canopied with alders, the river to the left, rhodies ranging up the hillside to the right.

Purple and white foxglove spires bloom all summer, and the salmonberries ripen to a deep orange color. Delicate, lacy blooms of ocean spray nods in the breeze, and even the thistles get in the act, flowering atop their thorny heads.

The road weaves through the lush forest, climbing steadily, passing little waterfalls, gaining grander westward views. Can you spot the ocean?

You'll pass a road to the right (FS 4890) leading to Goodwin Peak and one to the left (FS 4830) with a sign to Florence, but continue straight on what's now FS 5036, following the sign to Mapleton.

The road is paved again, heading downhill with more nice views. Power lines feed a radio array on Goodwin Peak. About 33 miles is the first encounter with Sweet Creek. Turn right on gravel FS 939 to Beaver Creek Falls and follow it to the parking area. A short trail to the falls gives just a taste of what you're in for. An interpretive sign explains the series of 11 waterfalls in this stretch of Sweet Creek.

Return to your vehicle, and then continue on the main road to Wagon Road Trail, a 0.8-mile stroll through luxuriant forest to two vista points. The wildlife here at certain times of the year includes a robust population of salamanders -- take care you don't squish any on the trail!

Continuing on the road, you'll come to the Sweet Creek Falls Trail, which offers a hike upriver to view the waterfalls you've seen from the previous hike, only from the other side of the river, and access to the

Waterfall at Sweet Creek, with catwalks in background

catwalk trail downriver.

The fourth access, Homestead Trail, is perhaps the best. There are restrooms and a picnic area. The river trail begins here, with the first stretch accessible for wheelchairs. The wonderful, mixed-species forest includes grand old firs, cedars and maples. After crossing a bridge and passing some beautiful river settings, the path encounters iron and wooden catwalks that lead to further waterfalls and riffles.

You might find a brochure at the interpretive sign that explains Sweet Creek was named for a pioneer family that settled here in 1876. Zara Sweet and his family were part of a 100-wagon migration from Illinois in the 1840s, and settled in Oregon City when the wagon train finally arrived in the west. Theirs was one of only *seven* wagons that remained after the harrowing, six-month trek.

The Sweets were later drawn to San Francisco by the Gold Rush excitement. But rather than chasing off into the foothills, Zara stayed in the city and built homes and wagons, and owned a blacksmith shop. After a number of moves, the family settled at Sweet Creek in 1876. In those days, this canyon — with its relatively easy grades over the rugged Coast Range — lay along a principal route from the Willamette Valley to the Siuslaw River and Florence.

The family farmed level patches of land along the canyon, and was among the first to begin logging the thickly-forested slopes. Many generations of loggers followed, harvesting hundreds of thousands of board feet of timber. These days, much of the forest has been replanted into a growing-back plantation of Douglas fir, and the sound of chainsaws and heavy equipment is rare. Few people venture into this neck of the woods, which is part of the Siuslaw National Forest, with a few patches of private holdings.

The Forest Service maintains Sweet Creek Trail as a day-use area, and has spared this part of the canyon from logging. Once you visit this place, you'll appreciate that bit of foresight.

When you're ready to move on, continue north on FS 5036. My suggested route will soon turn from this road and head back down through the woods, emerging near Woahink Lake and US 101 south of Florence.

You have another return option, however, which would take you to Mapleton and thence down Highway 38 to Florence. See map for details of that route.

Otherwise, about 1 mile from the Homestead Trailhead, turn left (sharply SW) on paved FS 24, following a sign to Florence, 19.

This lesser-traveled road heads uphill and seems to double back the way you've just come, then crests out and travels along ridges with big views west and south. Miles of back-country ensue.

Pass a road to Karnowski Ridge. At about mile 42, at a "T" intersection with a gravel spur to Elk Wallow Pit, bear right following the main paved FS 24.

Teh road descends. Bear right again at a "Y", following a sign to Florence. Pavement turns to gravel in a few miles, then pavement starts again as you skirt under powerlines. You go over a cattle guard and pass some houses; keep bearing right on the main road here, and at another "Y" at about mile 49, following signs to US 101.

You'll cross a couple of arms of Woahink Lake. There's a lovely lakeside picnic area, part of Honeyman State Park. And then here's US 101. Florence is a few miles north; turn left (S) to return to Coos Bay, about 50 miles.

Any questions?

29. How To Miss A Monsoon

A chapter on rainy day places seems appropriate enough when you consider an average year sees 60 inches of the stuff. That's a lot of rain!

Oddly, though, nary a drop falls in the months of July, August and September, and it's not unusual for dry conditions to take us to other extreme: fire danger. Your trip to the woods may not only be washed out, it may be canceled because of tinder-dry conditions.

This would seem hard to believe once you sit through a typical rainstorm on the coast, with water roaring sideways at 60 or 90 miles an hour for days on end.

Trees and power lines blow down, the fleet's tied up tight, but life pretty much goes on otherwise. Still, it's not much fun trying to make a tour. Even if the rain and wind lets up, where to go? Forest roads can be impassable because of downed trees and landslides. The valleys are flooded; even the Oregon Dunes can be soggy.

Winter can be a great time to check out the beach, especially on a rare, clear day after a storm. This is discussed in the chapter on beaches.

At the height of a storm, though, the beach can be treacherous, with high surf and driftwood logs tossed around like matchsticks. Stay off the beach during storms!

Another unfortunate weather phenomenon along the coast is the summer wind. It kicks up nearly every afternoon, and can really motivate folks toward indoor activities.

In other words, we've eliminated the outdoor adventures for the sake of this chapter. Now is the time to head indoors.

There are overlooked opportunities in all our little towns, even if it's just an old curiosity shop. Museums, galleries and shops are never really crowded, and practically deserted during the off-season.

If you are indeed visiting during winter, keep in mind some places are closed, or on a limited schedule.

Museums

We'll start in the "big city" of Coos Bay, with the Coos Art Museum, at 235 Anderson St. one block west of US 101. Constructed in 1936 as the town's post office, the building has Art Deco influences inside and out, and features changing and permanent displays. An upstairs room has memorabilia from legendary runner Steve Prefontaine, a Coos Bay native and 1970s-era Olympic contender. It's open 11 to 5, Tuesday to Saturday.

The Marshfield Sun was a pioneer newspaper, and this unusual five-sided building (moved from its original location) was its office. Publisher and editor Jesse Luce held sway for several decades with strong opinions about public affairs in Marshfield, as Coos Bay was called.

Now a museum, it's received material and printing equipment from

Coos Art Museum features Art Deco touches

many other places, and keeps regular hours in summer. It can be opened by special request in the off-season. The Bay Area Chamber of Commerce has more information.

Among the latest entries into the museum scene is the Oregon Coast Historical Railway, which currently doesn't have a museum *per se*, but displays a 1922 Baldwin steam locomotive and other equipment at their site along US 101 northbound in Coos Bay. The group hopes to eventually construct a museum/depot, and offer excursion rides.

North Bend is home of the Coos County Historical Society Museum, at least as of this writing. A new museum is planned for downtown Coos Bay, but until then, the facility is located along US 101 at the north end of North Bend, near the "Welcome to North Bend" sign. Exhibits change periodically. On permanent display are Indian and pioneer artifacts, from obsidian knives to a foot-powered milking machine. A hands-on exhibit of farmhouse gadgets is marked "please touch."

Hours are 10 to 4 Tuesday to Saturday. Right next to the museum is the North Bend Information Center, with a vast collection of promotional literature from throughout the western states and British Columbia. The staff and volunteers are a treasure-trove of local information.

The South Slough National Estuarine Research Reserve (discussed in chapter 3) has an interpretive center with interesting exhibits. And maybe the rain will let up enough for you to take the Ten-Minute Tour around the center.

Reedsport: Reedsport has transformed its historic old town district, putting utility wires underground, upgrading sidewalks and storefronts, and installing 1930s-era lights. Highlight is the Umpqua Discovery Center, in a modern building along the waterfront. A fascinating, multi-sensory exhibit called Tidewaters and Time includes diorama-type murals, interactive displays and a re-creation of a dock and shops along the Umpqua River in early-day Gardiner. Another part of the museum features a natural history display, also with interactive exhibits.

Winchester Bay: Just south of Reedsport is Winchester Bay, and the mouth of the Umpqua River. On a prominent hill above the bay is the Umpqua River Lighthouse, with tours of the light, built in the 1890s, and visitor center in one of the former Coast Guard buildings. It's open May 1 to Sept. 30.

Bandon: The Bandon Historical Society Museum occupies the town's former city hall, and is situated along US 101 at Filmore St., in the town's original city hall. This is another community with a rich history, cherished to this day by the many second, third and fourth-generation residents, and evident in the care given to museum exhibits. There are excellent permanent displays of the region's various industries and activities, from logging to dairy farming to fishing, with changing exhibits on specialized subjects.

Myrtle Point: One of my favorites is the Coos County Logging Museum in Myrtle Point, located at 7th and Maple Streets, just a block off Highway 42. Look for the "onion dome." It's open on a regular schedule in summer; contact city hall in the off-season.

The building was constructed in 1910 as a scaled-down replica of the Mormon Tabernacle in Salt Lake City. The acoustics of the tabernacle are exquisite, but unfortunately the sonic characteristics didn't translate into a smaller size, and the result in this small, domed building is best described as "acoustical chaos." There are weird "dead spots" in certain parts of the room, including directly in the middle. Try to make this tour with a friend (or two), and you'll have fun just talking to each other as you wander around!

Speaking of walking, you can take a walking tour of Myrtle Point trees. Not really a rainy day activity, but okay on a gloomy day. You can find a brochure about the walking tour in the Logging Museum, city hall and many businesses.

Florence: Housed in a building that once served as a pizza parlor and later a church, the Siuslaw Pioneer Museum is an absorbing conglomeration of fascinating artifacts and photos from Florence's early days. There are knowledgeable volunteers and staffers, and an extensive research library. Closed Mondays, New Year's Day, Easter, Thanksgiving and the month of December. Located on US 101 about 2 miles south of Florence.

Indoor Sports and Activities
Nearly all communities have private fitness centers, and many of them welcome (for a fee) one-time visitors. The Bay Area Athletic

Club, 985 Newmark Ave., in Coos Bay's Empire District, is among the largest, and features a swimming pool, racquetball courts, saunas, spas and other amenities. Another privately run enterprise in the downtown area of Coos Bay, called the Outdoor Inn, offers a play facility for youngsters.

The North Bend Swimming Pool -- an indoor pool -- has regular public swim hours. Coos Bay's public pool is outdoors -- 'tho heated -- in Mingus Park, and it, too, is open to the public at certain hours.

There's a bowling alley in North Bend, and a multi-screen movie theater adjacent to Pony Village Mall. Also in North Bend, along US 101 and the waterfront, is the Mill Casino, an Indian-run facility that offers machines and live-action games and nightly entertainment.

There are community theater groups in many South Coast towns -- *four* in the Coos Bay/ North Bend area -- which offer plays nearly every weekend evening of the year, and Sunday matinees.

The newly-built Sprague Theater in Bandon has shows and events year-'round, and Southwestern Oregon Community College has a new performing arts facility with a busy schedule of events. You can find schedules at visitor centers in each town.

Factory Tours

You can't go far without encountering a myrtlewood shop, and some of them are interesting because they do the work right on the premises.

Among the best known is the Oregon Connection, formerly the House of Myrtlewood, along US 101 at the south end of Coos Bay. It's actually a mini sawmill with a maxi gift shop attached. You can follow a self-guided tour that takes you through the mill and right down the middle of the "line." You also watch a few short videos along the way.

Peek into drying rooms stuffed full of hardwood slabs, which are 50 percent water when green. In another part of the mill, huge blades saw up logs that are stacked right out back. My favorite is the room full of spinning, belt-driven lathes. It's right out of the old days, with the belts traveling on pulleys directly overhead. In fact, this line is 80 years old, a real gem. The retail area displays some fine pieces of the elegantly grained wood. If it can be carved out of wood, rest assured they've tried it in myrtlewood. Test your expertise in the putting area with one of the golf clubs made with myrtlewood heads. There's even a room of "seconds" and small slabs for hobby woodcrafters.

Oh yeah, and they have an ice cream parlor in there, too. Don't all sawmills?

As far as the larger sawmills go, the days of factory tours are pretty much over. The timber companies do, however, sometimes offer summer tours of their "working woods" in conjunction with the Oregon State University Extension Service (541)-396-3121, ext. 240. Also inquire at the chamber of commerce or contact the timber companies; the top three are Menasha, Weyerhaeuser and Georgia-Pacific.

Bandon Cheese Factory along US 101 in Bandon is a favorite place to visit in any weather. You can sample many varieties of cheeses, and watch a video on cheese making. A glass window looks onto the cheese factory, and you can often observe workers busy with the process.

In Old Town Bandon (and in Coos Bay's Empire district) is Cranberry Sweets, which makes an assortment of sweets on the premises.

Big Wheel General Store in Old Town Bandon is "home of the fudge factory," with candy and other treats.

The exquisite art of glass blowing can be viewed at Bandon Glass Art studio on US 101 across from the Bandon Visitors Center. There's another art glass studio south of Bandon along US 101.

About 4 miles south of Bandon on US 101 is Wildlife Game Park, with a gamut of exotic and domesticated animals for petting and observation. Fun in any weather, although they close in winter.

Shipping news

Maritime commerce has always been a vital part of the region, and watching the comings and goings of the fishing fleet and oceangoing freighters is always interesting. One of the best places to watch big ships tie up is near the Roseburg Lumber Co. dock on Coos Bay's North Spit. The daily newspaper has a schedule of ship arrivals and departures, or you can call the Port of Coos Bay for information.

In Charleston, the US Coast Guard station can be toured by calling the public affairs officer at 756-9669.

On another maritime topic, there's a tour boat called *Rendezvous* that berths at the Coos Bay Boardwalk. They have regular bay tours and outings on special occasions; find out more by calling (541) 267-5661 or by checking at the boat.

The Old . . . and New

Since I mentioned curio shops earlier, here's a plug for downtown North Bend, which may have the greatest concentration of collectibles in Coos County. The shops are great fun to browse through and the owners won't mind if you don't buy something every time, "just once in a while."

It's handy that they're all in the same neighborhood, too, on and around Sherman Avenue, which is US 101 South. This is also where you find several used bookstores and a natural foods co-op.

North Bend also boasts Pony Village Mall, largest enclosed mall on the Oregon Coast. It's on Virginia Avenue about a half-mile west of US 101.

Libraries are a great rainy day retreat, and both Coos Bay and North Bend have excellent facilities. There are the usual resources, including computers with Internet access. Both have displays of art that change on a regular basis, and offer presentations, children's' shows and other special events.

Southwestern Oregon Community College also operates a library on its Newmark Avenue campus. There are lots of books — many technical volumes — but it's not as fun to browse or hang out in. As noted, the college has a new performing arts center with a full schedule of events.

Reedsport, Bandon, Port Orford, Coquille and Myrtle Point all boast libraries that are vital places, serving not just as repositories of knowledge, but as gathering places for locals of all ages, and as clearinghouses of information, both scholarly and gossipy. A warmth unique to the small town.

Appendix A

Lookout & Recreation Rentals in the South Coast Region

The US Forest Service offers decommissioned fire watchtowers as overnight rentals in national forests throughout the west, and the Siskiyou National Forest has joined the action in recent years with a number of opportunities. Some ranger districts have other rentals ranging from secluded tents to large cabins.

The best way to get up-to-date information is via their website, *www.fs.fed.us/r6/siskiyou/rental.htm.* There are write-ups and photos of all the offerings. The most popular is Snow Camp Lookout, on the Chetco Ranger District. It was the first rental in the region, and the fact that it's "at grade" (no stairs to climb) makes it popular. There's even a book about it, called *View With A Room*, by David Calahan.

There's another, Quail Prairie, on the Chetco district, and they also manage one on the Gold Beach Ranger District called Lake Of the Woods. The Powers Ranger District has Bald Knob Lookout. They're available from Memorial Day weekend to Oct. 31, depending on weather. The ranger district offices begin taking reservations on the first working day of the new year, and weekends are often booked up for the entire season *within a matter of hours!* So if you want to do this, start planning ahead. Rates range from $35 to $50 per night.

Some of the lookouts – many, in fact – are considered primitive camping experiences. At most of them, you get a single bed, a pot-bellied stove and a view. You bring everything from wood for the stove, to bedding and provisions, and lots of water.

A few are better equipped. Among them are Lake of the Woods and Bald Knob. They have propane-fueled refrigerator, cookstove and oven, heater and lamps. Lake of the Woods even has a double bed! (You still have to bring bedding, provisions and water.) Outhouses are a few hundred feet from the base of the towers.

You can drive right up to the base of both. Bald Knob, 20 feet above the ground, has two flights of stairs to negotiate, while at 10 feet Lake of the Woods has just a single flight.

Lake of the Woods even boasts a "solar shower" – a 5-gallon black plastic jug set out in the sun, then hung up in the fiberglass shower stall (a remnant of the days when this was an active lookout.) Former visitors have left lots of homey touches at Lake of the Woods, even a guitar. There are visitor logs at the lookouts that are a lot of fun to read.

If you decide to stay at a lookout, the Forest Service will send information and helpful tips about what to bring, how to get there, and so on. One thing you might think about are moon phases. Stargazing is better when the moon isn't full (or doesn't rise until the wee hours of the morning), and a full moon can keep some light sleepers awake. (You're

Wild rhododendrons surround Bald Knob Lookout, now available as an overnight rental from Memorial Day weekend to October 31.

in a glass house, remember.) So consider consulting a calendar with moon phases when scheduling your nights on the mountaintop. Otherwise get ready for an experience you'll always remember.

Appendix B

What's Happening to the Trees?

Whether you're traveling along main roads or backcountry byways, you might notice what seems to be an alarming number of trees dead, dying or looking unwell. For a variety of unfortunate reasons, our trees are under attack by diseases.

Some of the diseases are confined to a single species, while others are afflicting a disturbingly wide range of trees and shrubs. Many diseases kill their hosts; another merely slows growth. Research has produced some promising results, but in other cases scientists and foresters have not come up with a viable defense.

Douglas fir

Swiss needle cast, *phaeocryptopus gaeumannii*, was first described in 1928 as it devastated Douglas fir stands in Switzerland. Attacking only Douglas fir, airborne spores spread to Germany, Austria and Czechoslovakia. By 1939, it was found from northern California to British Columbia, but wasn't thought to affect tree health. In the 1980s, a few stands of Coast Range Douglas fir tainted by Swiss Needle Cast began showing chlorosis, a sort of bleaching of the needles. Also affected were commercial Christmas tree plantations.

Great swaths of trees take on a yellowish pallor -- the "cast" -- in late winter and early spring, and have noticeably less needle retention. The pathogen is manifested on the underside of the needle, where you can see black, fruiting nodes.

Aerial surveys in 2001 revealed more than 221,000 acres touched by the disease, almost exclusively in a 12-mile-wide "fog belt" along the coastline. Researchers speculate that a number of factors are at work. The fungus seems to thrive in the relatively warm, moist climate. Many seedlings used for replanting came from inland or higher-elevation plantations, where trees may have more naturally-occurring mechanisms of disease tolerance. In addition, the formerly mixed forests of fir, Sitka spruce, cedar and western hemlock, among other trees, have been logged and replanted exclusively into Douglas fir, perhaps also weakening natural disease tolerance.

While Swiss Needle Cast slows growth, it doesn't kill trees. Fungicides are available for commercial Christmas tree farms, and foresters and landowners are being advised to carefully select seedlings, plant other species of trees, or create plantations of mixed species.

Port Orford Cedars and Sudden Oak Death

One of the most notorious tree diseases has been attacking and killing the prized Port Orford cedar, or white cedar, for many decades. Called *phytophthora lateralis*, it was first reported in ornamental cedars near Seattle in 1923 and thought to have come from imported Asian varieties. By 1952 it was found in southwestern Oregon, where young cedar abounds on wild and cutover lands. Spread by water- and mudborne spores that infect the roots, a thread-like fungus slowly "dries out" the tree. A slightly wilting appearance eventually becomes a coppery pallor; in the final stage the tree is a light-brown skeleton. "Resting" spores lurk in soil and decomposed roots awaiting a chance to move on.

They spread via earth movement in construction, road building, logging operations and by livestock, game animals and humans. The spores can also move through surface water.

Phytophthora diseases can be suppressed by fungicides, but not actually eliminated, so the best defense for many years has been to limit the spread of the disease and protect uninfected stands. In some places, operators of construction and logging equipment must wash off equipment -- especially tires and tractor treads -- before leaving infected areas. Visitors in autos and trucks must do the same. Many former logging spurs and side roads have been closed to protect healthy stands.

Research continues, with successful plantings of disease-resistant Port

Orford cedars. Still unaffected are other cedars, such as red cedar, which grows profusely in the Coast Range and along the coast.

In an unfortunate turn of events, a close relative of the pathogen, *phytophtora ramorum*, has been blamed for what's called Sudden Oak Death syndrome in California. In addition to infecting the mighty oaks, it's killing broad-leaved trees and shrubs such as rhododendron, evergreen huckleberry, madrone, myrtle, black oak, big-leaf maple and manzanita.

In the oaks, the mobile spores invade through the bark, causing oozing cankers that weaken the tree and invite boring insects. In other species, it's believed the disease attacks through the leaves.

The disease moved north, making an appearance in southwestern Oregon in 2001 and alarming foresters and landowners already battling tree diseases. A total of nine sites in Curry County, northeast of Brookings, were found to contain the pathogen. Infected trees and brush were cut and burned, and hundreds of other samples were collected from other sites, and as of spring 2002, the tests have come back negative.

While the picture can be discouraging, residents and visitors to the region can do their part by following any guidelines or travel restrictions set up to slow or stop the spread of diseases.

(Information for this section provided by Oregon State University Swiss Needle Cast Cooperative and the US Forest Service. An Internet search of these topics will provide an abundance of additional material.)

Other Recreational Opportunities

This book is merely a slice of the region's recreational pie. There are dozens of other places to check out, from small city parks to obscure back roads, not to mention all the waterways. Opportunities abound. You can rent a bicycle, canoe, dune buggy or kayak, or take a windsurfing class, or go for a horseback ride. There are charter boats for freshwater and ocean fishing, as well as guided nature excursions.

Miscellaneous Places
Winchester Trail System offers 30 miles of single-track trails and gravel roads for off-road ("dirt") motorcycles and mountain bicycles. Many challenging hills, with lots of potholes, exposed tree roots and rutted sections. Trails are marked with milepost-like systems, and numbered 1 to 22 (although not all are marked.) You can obtain a map of the trails from bicycle shops in the Bay Area (listed below) or from the Coos Region Trails Partnership's website, www.coostrails.com. The trail system is 12 miles south of Coos Bay along US 101, at milepost 251. There's a sign at the staging area with more information.

Euphoria Ridge Trails, on BLM land near Bridge (east of Myrtle Point), offers 12 miles of gravel roads and single-track trails for mountain bicyclists. You can obtain maps from bike shops and the BLM office in North Bend, or from the Coos Region Trails Partnership website listed above. To get there, go east on Highway 42. Bridge is 9 miles east of Myrtle Point; turn left (N) on Big Creek Rd. and follow signs to trail system.

Disc (i.e., Frisbee) Golf Courses: Simpson Park, North Bend and Mingus Park, Coos Bay. Both courses have 18 "holes" (baskets).

Outfitters and Rentals

Boating: The excursion boat *Rendezvous* offers cruises on Coos Bay (541) 267-5661. The famous jet-boat trips on Rogue River in Gold Beach are offered by Jerry's Rogue River Jet Boats (800) 451-3645 and Mail Boat Hydro-Jet Boats (800) 458-3511.

Bicycling: High Tide Rental, Charleston, has bikes for rent (541) 888-3664. Bike sales and service at Moe's Bikes in North Bend (541) 756-7536 and Bay Area Bicycle Center, North Bend (541) 756-4522.

Diving: Sunset Sports in Pony Village Mall, North Bend, (541) 756-3483, has sales and rentals.

Dune buggy/ATVs: FarWest 4 Wheel Rental, North Bend (541) 756-3491; Pacific Coast Recreation, North Bend (541) 756-7183; Spinreel Rentals, Hauser (541) 759-3313; Winchester Bay Dune Buggy, Winchester Bay (541) 271-6972; Dune Country ATV, Winchester Bay (541) 271-9357; Sand Dunes Frontier, Florence (541) 997-3544; Sandland Adventure, Florence (541) 997-8087.

Fishing: Betty Kay Charters in trips for rockfish and halibut (in season) March-October (541) 888-4241. River's End Guide Service in Winchester Bay offers freshwater and ocean fishing excursions (888) 388-3125. Also in Winchester Bay is Strike Zone (800) 230-5350, with ocean fishing. There are a handful of guides in Gold Beach; call Curry Guide Association, (541) 247-3476.

Horseback riding: Family Four Stables, Coos Bay (541) 267-5301. Walking Hills, Coos Bay (541) 267-2543; Bandon Beach Stables, Bandon (541) 347-3423; C&M Stables, Florence (541) 997-7540.

Nature Tour: Wavecrest Discoveries offers guided nature tours with knowledgeable expert Marty Giles: driving, walking, kayaking, even clamming! Trips range from several hours to all day. (541) 267-4027.

Paddling: Adventure Kayak, Old Town Bandon, has rentals and tours (541) 347-3480. High Tide Rental, Charleston (541) 888-3664, has kayaks and one canoe for rent. Central Coast Watersports, Florence, (541) 997-7540, has kayak rentals. Sunset Sports in Pony Village Mall, North Bend, (541) 756-3483, sells kayaks and supplies.

Surfing/Windsurfing: Rocky Point Surf Shop, Coos Bay (541) 266-9020; Big Air Windsurfing, Langlois (541) 347-2692; Floras Lake Windsurfing, Langlois (541) 348-9912.

For Your Information

Bay Area Chamber of Commerce, Coos Bay (541) 269-0215
North Bend Info Center, North Bend (541) 756-4613
Coos County Parks Dept., Coquille 396-3121 x354
Oregon Dunes National Rec. Area, Reedsport (541) 271-3611
US Forest Service, Mapleton District, Florence (541) 902-3611
US Forest Service, Powers District, Powers (541) 439-3011
US Forest Service, Gold Beach District, Gold Beach (541) 247-2133
US Forest Service, Chetco District, Brookings (541) 469-2196
US Bureau of Land Management, North Bend (541) 756-0100
BLM Loon Lake Recreation Site (541) 599-2254
BLM Roseburg (541) 440-4931
BLM Eugene (541) 683-6600
Oregon Dept of Forestry, Coos Bay (541) 267-4136
Oregon State Parks, Southwestern Div., Coos Bay (541) 888-8867
Douglas County Parks Dept., Winchester Bay (541) 271-4631
Port of Coos Bay Charleston Marina (541) 888-2548
South Slough Estuarine Reserve, Charleston (541) 888-5558
Bandon Visitor Center, Old Town Bandon (541) 347-9616
City of North Bend (541) 756-4613
City of Coos Bay (541) 269-8918
City of Bandon (541) 347-2437
Myrtle Point Chamber of Commerce (541) 572-2626
Coquille Chamber of Commerce (541) 396-3414
Lakeside Chamber of Commerce (541) 759-3981
Powers Chamber of Commerce (541) 439-3508
Menasha Corp. Forest Tours (summers only) (541)756-1193
Marine weather (541) 888-3102
Aviation weather (541) 657-0135
Continuous weather info on VHF: 162.4 mHz
Web sites: *www.coostrails.com*
　　　　　 www.oregonsbayarea.com
　　　　　 www.or.blm.gov/coosbay

Acknowledgments and Suggested Reading

Pioneer History of Coos & Curry Counties, O.O. Dodge
Oregon Geographic Names, Lewis A. McArthur
Pioneers & Incidents of the Upper Coquille Valley, A.H. Wooldridge
South Slough Adventures, Friends of the South Slough
The Baltimore Colony & Pioneer Recollections, Binger Hermann
Myrtle Point Beginnings, Curt Beckham

Oregon South Coast History, Nathan Douthit
Exploring the Wild Oregon Coast, Bonnie Henderson
100 Hikes/Trail Guide Oregon Coast, William Sullivan
50 Hikes in Oregon's Coast Range and Siskiyous, R&G Ostertag
Coos Bay, The Pioneer Period 1851-1890, Stephen D. Beckham
Land of the Umpqua, A Douglas County History, S. Beckham
Above the Falls, Lionel Youst
She's Tricky Like Coyote, Lionel Youst
Tioga's Pigs, E.A. Krewson
100 Hikes/Trail Guide Oregon Coast, William Sullivan
50 Hikes in Oregon's Coast Range and Siskiyous, R&G Ostertag
The Night Bandon Burned, Dow Beckham
The Northwest Coast, A Natural History, Stewart T. Schultz
Driving the Pacific Coast, Oregon, Kenn Oberrecht
Oregon Coastal Access Guide, Kenn Oberrecht
Oregon's Coos Region Canoe & Kayak Guide, Ron Wardman

About the Author

Tom Baake has been writing about and photographing the region since the early 1980s, when he was editor of the North Bend *News*. His column in the newspaper *Prime Time* inspired this book, and he's written for publications ranging from *American Machinist* to *Oregon Coast* to *The Physician and Sportsmedicine*. His series about sawmill closures in the Coquille Valley *Sentinel* won top honors from the Oregon Newspaper Publishers Association, and he has contributed to books on computer technology, solar heating, kayaking and sportsmedicine.

Now available at book stores and gift shops . . .

Oregon's Coos Region Canoe & Kayak Guide

A complete guidebook to local paddling opportunities!